Welcome!
to Georgia Social Studies

Dear Georgia Student,

Who has made Georgia a great state? In this book you will read about people such as James Oglethorpe, Sequoyah, and Martin Luther King, Jr. You will learn about how they lived and the important events in their lives.

As you read, you will meet your learning goals, which are listed on the pages that follow. The learning you do this year in social studies will be yours for the rest of your life!

You are on your way!

GEORGIA

Georgia Performance Standards
GRADE 2

Historical Understandings

SS2H1 The student will read about and describe the lives of historical figures in Georgia history.

> **a.** Identify the contributions made by these historic figures: James Oglethorpe, Tomochichi, and Mary Musgrove (founding of Georgia); Sequoyah (development of a Cherokee alphabet); Jackie Robinson (sports); Martin Luther King, Jr. (civil rights); Jimmy Carter (leadership and human rights).
>
> **b.** Describe how everyday life of these historical figures is similar to and different from everyday life in the present (food, clothing, homes, transportation, communication, recreation, rights, and freedoms).

SS2H2 The student will describe the Georgia Creek and Cherokee cultures of the past in terms of tools, clothing, homes, ways of making a living, and accomplishments.

> **a.** Describe the regions in Georgia where the Creek and Cherokee lived and how the people used their local resources.
>
> **b.** Compare and contrast the Georgia Creek and Cherokee cultures of the past to Georgians today.

Geographic Understandings

SS2G1 The student will locate major topographical features of Georgia and will describe how these features define Georgia's surface.

a. Locate all the geographic regions of Georgia: Blue Ridge Mountains, Piedmont, Coastal Plain, Valley and Ridge, and Appalachian Plateau.

b. Locate the major rivers: Ocmulgee, Oconee, Altamaha, Savannah, St. Mary's, Chattahoochee, and Flint.

SS2G2 The student will describe the cultural and geographic systems associated with the historical figures in SS2H1 and Georgia's Creek and Cherokee.

a. Identify specific locations significant to the life and times of each historic figure on a political map.

b. Describe how place (physical and human characteristics) had an impact on the lives of each historic figure.

c. Describe how each historic figure adapted to and was influenced by his/her environment.

d. Trace examples of travel and movement of these historic figures and their ideas across time.

e. Describe how the region in which these historic figures lived affected their lives and compare these regions to the region in which the students live.

Government/Civic Understandings

SS2CG1 The student will define the concept of government and the need for rules and laws.

SS2CG2 The student will identify the roles of the following elected officials:

a. President (leader of our nation)

b. Governor (leader of our state)

c. Mayor (leader of a city)

SS2CG3 The student will give examples of how the historic figures under study demonstrate the positive citizenship traits of honesty, dependability, liberty, trustworthiness, honor, civility, good sportsmanship, patience, and compassion.

SS2CG4 The student will demonstrate knowledge of the state and national capitol buildings by identifying them from pictures and capitals of the United States of America (Washington, D.C.) and the state of Georgia (Atlanta) by locating them on appropriate maps.

Economic Understandings

SS2E1 The student will explain that because of *scarcity*, people must make *choices* and incur *opportunity costs*.

SS2E2 The student will identify ways in which goods and services are *allocated* (by price; majority rule; contests; force; sharing; lottery; command; first-come, first-served; personal characteristics; and others).

SS2E3 The student will explain that people usually use money to obtain the goods and services they want and explain how money makes trade easier than barter.

SS2E4 The student will describe the *costs* and *benefits* of personal *spending* and *saving* choices.

HOUGHTON MIFFLIN
SOCIAL STUDIES

★ OUR STATE ★

Visit **Education Place®**
www.eduplace.com/kids

HOUGHTON MIFFLIN   BOSTON

GEORGIA

★ AUTHORS ★

Senior Author
Dr. Herman J. Viola
Curator Emeritus
Smithsonian Institution

Dr. Cheryl Jennings
Project Director
Florida Institute of
    Education
University of North
    Florida

Dr. Sarah Witham
Bednarz
Associate Professor,
    Geography
Texas A&M University

Dr. Mark C. Schug
Professor and Director
Center for Economic
    Education
University of Wisconsin,
    Milwaukee

Dr. Carlos E. Cortés
Professor Emeritus, History
University of California,
Riverside

Dr. Charles S. White
Associate Professor
School of Education
Boston University

Georgia Program Consultant
Glen Blankenship

Consulting Authors

Dr. Dolores Beltran
Assistant Professor
Curriculum Instruction
California State University, Los Angeles
(Support for English Language Learners)

Dr. MaryEllen Vogt
Co-Director
California State University Center
for the Advancement of Reading
(Reading in the Content Area)

HOUGHTON MIFFLIN
SOCIAL STUDIES

★ OUR STATE ★

HOUGHTON MIFFLIN   BOSTON

GEORGIA

Consultants

Philip J. Deloria
Associate Professor
Department of History
and Program in
American Studies
University of Michigan

Lucien Ellington
Professor of Education
and Asia Program
Co-Director
University of Tennessee,
Chattanooga

Thelma Wills Foote
Associate Professor
University of California,
Irvine

Stephen J. Fugita
Distinguished Professor
Psychology and Ethnic
Studies
Santa Clara University

Charles C. Haynes
Senior Scholar
First Amendment Center

Ted Hemmingway
Professor of History
The Florida Agricultural &
Mechanical University

Douglas Monroy
Professor of History
The Colorado College

Lynette K. Oshima
Assistant Professor
Department of Language,
Literacy and Sociocultural
Studies and Social Studies
Program Coordinator
University of New Mexico

Jeffrey Strickland
Assistant Professor, History
University of Texas Pan
American

Clifford E. Trafzer
Professor of History and
American Indian Studies
University of California,
Riverside

Georgia Program Consultant

Glen Blankenship

Teacher Reviewers

Sharon Blount
Meadowbrook
North Kansas City, MO

Jane Cregg
Mendell Elementary
Roxbury, MA

Bonnie Ewing
Ideal Elementary
Countryside, IL

Elizabeth Farrar
Bella Vista School
Bella Vista, CA

Carol Hancock
Kedron Elementary
Peachtree City, GA

Diana Hendricks
Davis Elementary
Columbus, GA

Lori Martinez
Woodland Charter
Elementary
Atlanta, GA

Kathleen Mastaby
Mendell Elementary
Roxbury, MA

Shari Moleterno
Jefferson School
Berwyn, IL

Fred Richardson
West Zephyrhills Elementary
Zephyrhills, FL

Phyllis Yamaguchi
Alvarado Elementary
Signal Hill, CA

Donna Zaccaria
William Cramp Elementary
Philadelphia, PA

Printed in the U.S.A.

ISBN-13: 978-0-618-49786-7
ISBN-10: 0-618-49786-2

6789 DW 13 12 11 10 09 08

Contents

Introduction

Bringing the world to your classroom!

UNIT 2 Georgia's Places 74

Vocabulary Preview
Reading Strategies: Question, Monitor/Clarify 76

UNIT 3 Georgia at Work 124

Vocabulary Preview
Reading Strategies: Question, Summarize 126

UNIT 4 America's Government

162

Vocabulary Preview
Reading Strategies: Summarize, Question 164

9

References

Resources

Extend Lessons

Connect the core lesson to an important concept and dig into it. Extend your social studies knowledge!

Biography   GPS Biography

More biographies at www.eduplace.com/kids/hmss/

Readers' Theater

Citizenship

Primary Source

More primary sources at www.eduplace.com/kids/hmss/

Geography

Literature

Economics

History

Skill Lessons

Take a step-by-step approach to learning and practicing key social studies skills.

Map and Globe Skills

Graph and Chart Skills

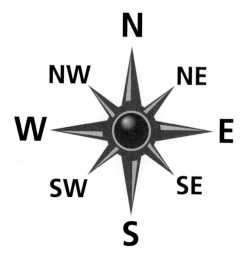

Visual Learning

Maps, graphs, and charts help you learn.

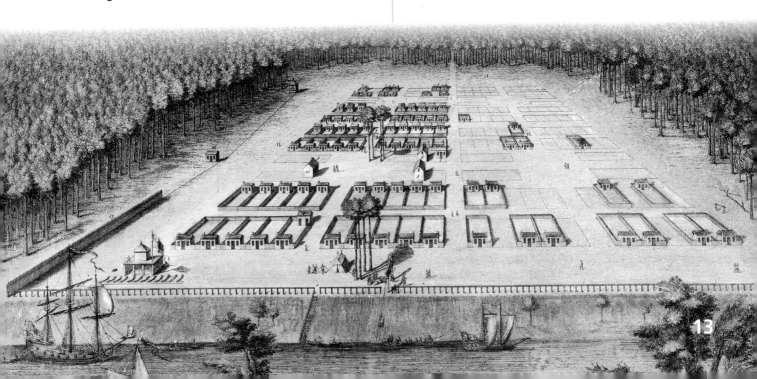

About Your Textbook

❶ How It's Organized

Units The major sections of your book are units. Each starts with a big idea.

Explore big ideas in geography, history, economics, government, and culture.

Get ready for reading.

Each unit opens with a vocabulary preview.

Four important concepts get you started.

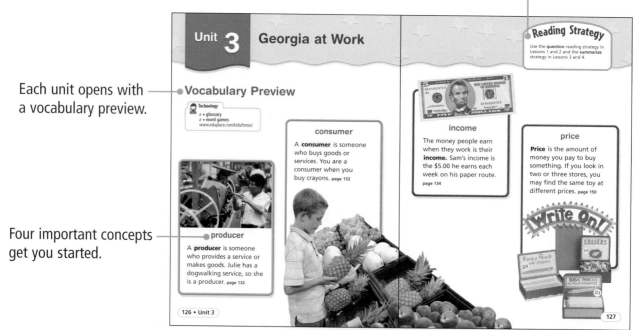

❷ Core and Extend

Lessons The lessons in your book have two parts: core and extend.

Core Lessons

Lessons bring social studies to life and help you meet your state's standards.

Core Lesson 3

Extend Lessons

Go deep into an important topic.

Extend
Primary Source

Core Lesson

Core Lesson 1

Where You Live

Vocabulary lists give you the words you need to know.

▶ **Vocabulary**
nation
state
continent

Reading skills support your understanding of the text.

⟳ **Reading Skill**
Classify

STANDARDS

Core
Geographic Understanding,
GPS: Map and Globe Skill 6: information from maps

Extend
GPS: Map and Globe Skill 1: cardinal directions

Build on What You Know
What do you call the community where you live? Do you know the rest of your address?

States in a Country
Carlos is going to mail a letter to his cousin Len. Len lives on Green Street in the city of Columbus. Carlos has written that address on the envelope.

return address

stamp

address

Carlos

78 • Unit 2

Before you read, use your prior knowledge.

Main ideas are underlined to show you what is important.

The United States is on the continent of North America. The United States shares North America with two other large nations. They are Canada and Mexico. Seven small nations south of Mexico and many island nations are part of North America too.

ATLANTIC OCEAN

Which oceans touch North America?

As you read, check your understanding.

Review What is one way that Mexico and the United States are alike?

Lesson Review

❶ **Vocabulary** Write a sentence that tells where you live. Use the words **nation, state,** and **continent** in the sentence.

❷ **Main Idea** What are the earth's seven continents?

✏ ▶ **Activity** Draw an envelope for a letter to a friend. Write your address and your friend's address on it.

After you read, check what you have learned.

81

Extend Lesson Learn more about an important topic.

Dig in and extend your knowledge.

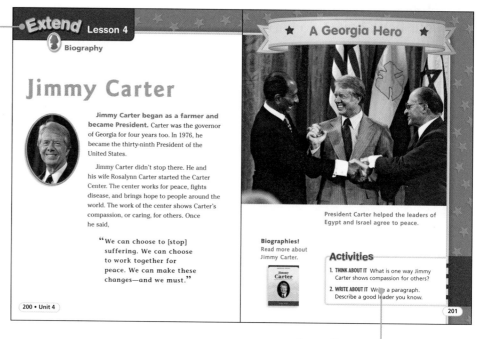

Extend Lesson 4
Biography

Jimmy Carter

Jimmy Carter began as a farmer and became President. Carter was the governor of Georgia for four years too. In 1976, he became the thirty-ninth President of the United States.

Jimmy Carter didn't stop there. He and his wife Rosalynn Carter started the Carter Center. The center works for peace, fights disease, and brings hope to people around the world. The work of the center shows Carter's compassion, or caring, for others. Once he said,

"We can choose to [stop] suffering. We can choose to work together for peace. We can make these changes—and we must."

200 • Unit 4

★ A Georgia Hero ★

President Carter helped the leaders of Egypt and Israel agree to peace.

Biographies! Read more about Jimmy Carter.

Jimmy Carter

Activities

1. **THINK ABOUT IT** What is one way Jimmy Carter shows compassion for others?
2. **WRITE ABOUT IT** Write a paragraph. Describe a good leader you know.

201

Write, talk, draw, and role-play!

Look for literature, readers' theater, geography, economics—and more.

Extend Lesson 3
Literature

A Cherokee Legend

Between Earth & Sky

A legend is a story that is told and retold over many, many years. Joseph Bruchac retold this Cherokee legend about **mountains** in Georgia and other southern states.

If we should travel
far to the South,
there in the land
of mountains and mist,
we might hear the story
of how Earth was first shaped.

Water Beetle came out
to see if it was ready,
but the ground was
still as wet as a swamp,
too soft for anyone to stand.

Great Buzzard said, "I will help dry the land."
He began to fly close above the new Earth.
Where his wings came down,
valleys were formed,
and where his wings lifted,
hills rose up through the mist.

So the many rolling valleys and hills
of that place called the Great Smokies
came into being there.

LITERATURE

Activities

1. **Talk About It** How does the Cherokee legend say that valleys were formed?
2. **Write About It** Make up a story about how another landform came to be.

56 • Unit 1

57

③ Skills

Skill Building Learn map, graph, and study skills, as well as citizenship skills for life.

Practice and apply each social studies skill.

Skill lessons step it out.

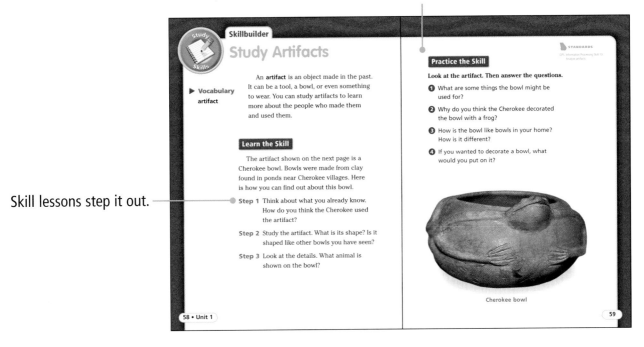

④ References

Citizenship Handbook

The back of your book includes sections you'll refer to again and again.

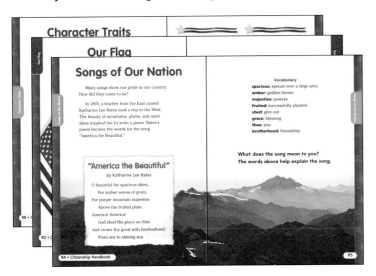

Resources

Look for atlas maps, a glossary of social studies terms, and an index.

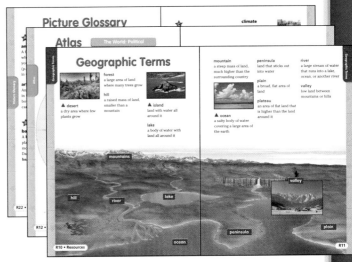

Reading Social Studies

Your book can help you be a successful reader. Here's what you will find:

VOCABULARY SUPPORT

Preview Learn four important words from the unit.

Lesson Vocabulary Learn the meanings of lesson vocabulary.

Vocabulary Practice Reuse words in the reviews, skills, and extends. Show that you know your vocabulary.

READING STRATEGIES

Look through your book and find the reading strategies at the beginning of each unit.

Predict and Infer

Monitor and Clarify

Question

Summarize

Unit **4** America's Government

Reading Strategy
Use the **summarize** reading strategy in Lessons 1, 2, and 3 and the **question** strategy in Lessons 4 and 5.

Vocabulary Preview

Technology
e • glossary
e • word games
www.eduplace.com/kids/hmss/

citizen
A **citizen** is a member of a community, state, or country. You are a citizen of your class too. page 188

government
A **government** needs a leader and a group of people who work together to run a community, state, or nation. page 168

election
An **election** is a time when people vote. You can hold a class election to make a choice. page 196

Constitution
The **Constitution** is a plan for making rules for the United States government. page 202

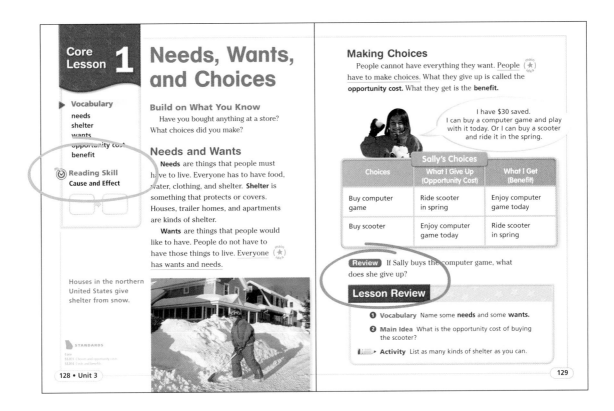

Core Lesson 1

Needs, Wants, and Choices

Vocabulary
needs
shelter
wants
opportunity cost
benefit

Reading Skill
Cause and Effect

Build on What You Know

Have you bought anything at a store? What choices did you make?

Needs and Wants

Needs are things that people must have to live. Everyone has to have food, water, clothing, and shelter. **Shelter** is something that protects or covers. Houses, trailer homes, and apartments are kinds of shelter.

Wants are things that people would like to have. People do not have to have those things to live. Everyone has wants and needs.

Houses in the northern United States give shelter from snow.

STANDARDS
Core
SS2E1 Choices and opportunity costs
SS2E2 Costs and benefits

128 • Unit 3

Making Choices

People cannot have everything they want. People have to make choices. What they give up is called the **opportunity cost**. What they get is the **benefit**.

I have $30 saved. I can buy a computer game and play with it today. Or I can buy a scooter and ride it in the spring.

Sally's Choices

Choices	What I Give Up (Opportunity Cost)	What I Get (Benefit)
Buy computer game	Ride scooter in spring	Enjoy computer game today
Buy scooter	Enjoy computer game today	Ride scooter in spring

Review If Sally buys the computer game, what does she give up?

Lesson Review

1 Vocabulary Name some **needs** and some **wants**.

2 Main Idea What is the opportunity cost of buying the scooter?

Activity List as many kinds of shelter as you can.

129

READING SKILLS

As you read, use the reading skills to organize the information.

Sequence

Cause and Effect

Compare and Contrast

Draw Conclusions

Predict Outcomes

Classify

Main Idea and Details

COMPREHENSION SUPPORT

Build on What You Know
Ask yourself what you know about the lesson topic. You may already know a lot!

Review Questions
Answer questions as you read. Did you understand what you read?

Social Studies
Why It Matters

Social Studies is exciting and fun. It is not just a book you read in school. You will use what you learn all your life.

WHEN I
► look around my neighborhood
► or read a map—
I'll use geography!

WHEN I
► save money or
► decide what to buy—
I'll use economics!

WHEN I
- go to a neighborhood meeting
- or decide who to vote for—
I'll use what I've learned about citizenship!

WHEN I
- hear the story of a person from the past
- read books and visit museums
- look closely at the world around me—
I'll think about history!

Georgia Is Our State

What makes Georgia a great place to live? It's the people, of course. Georgia's people are as different as the places where they live. Georgia is a great state!

Georgia Is Our State

In this book you will read about the people shown below. A biography book tells even more about each person. You will find out how these people made a difference to our country and our state.

Tomochichi
1644?–1739

He helped start a colony in Georgia.

James Oglethorpe
1696–1785

He wanted to help people start new lives in Georgia.

Mary Musgrove
1700?–1763

She helped Oglethorpe and Tomochichi talk to each other.

Biographies!
You will read about these heroes from Georgia's past.

Sequoyah
1801–1846

He made a Cherokee alphabet.

Jackie Robinson
1919–1972

He was the first African American major league baseball player.

Martin Luther King, Jr.
1929–1968

He worked for fair treatment for African Americans.

Jimmy Carter
1924–

He was President of the United States from 1977 to 1981.

UNIT 1

Georgia's Past

"**The world is full of stories, and from time to time they permit themselves to be told.**"

—Old Cherokee Saying

The Big Idea

Why is the past important to you today?

Unit 1 — Georgia's Past

Vocabulary Preview

Technology

e • glossary
e • word games
www.eduplace.com/kids/hmss/

history

We learn about people and events of the past when we read **history**. page 30

river

The Savannah **River** flows along the eastern side of Georgia. page 31

Reading Strategy

Use the **monitor and clarify** reading strategy in Lessons 1 and 2 and the **predict and infer** strategy in Lessons 3 and 4.

colonist

A **colonist** is a person who lives in a colony. Many colonists came to America seeking freedom.

page 42

ancestor

Someone in your family who lived before you were born is your **ancestor.**

page 64

Vocabulary

history
river

Reading Skill

Main Idea and Details

STANDARDS

SS2H2.a How the Creek used resources
SS2G2.b How place impacted the Creek

The Creek lived in this area near the Ocmulgee River.

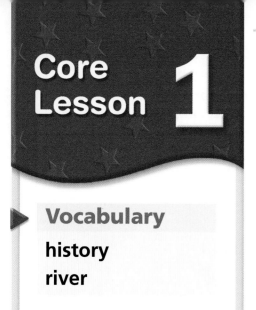

Creek wooden spoon

The Creek

Build on What You Know

How many different ways of using water can you name? The Creek people used water in some of the same ways you use it.

Georgia's First People

The Creek were one of the groups of American Indians that long ago lived in what is now Georgia. Other groups were the Timucua (tihm uh KOH uh) and the Cherokee. Their stories are part of Georgia's history. **History** is everything people can know about the past.

main idea

Where the Creek Lived

main idea

The Creek lived in many parts of Georgia. They usually built their towns and villages along rivers such as the Ocmulgee (ohk MUHL gee). A **river** is a large body of moving water that flows into another body of water. The Creek fished in the rivers and traveled on them in canoes.

The river water gathered dirt as it moved along. Sometimes the rivers flooded. When the water drained back into the rivers, the dirt was left behind. This new layer of rich dirt helped plants to grow in the Creek gardens.

Review What is one way that the Creek used rivers?

This map shows where the Creek lived in what is now Georgia. The Creek also lived in nearby states.

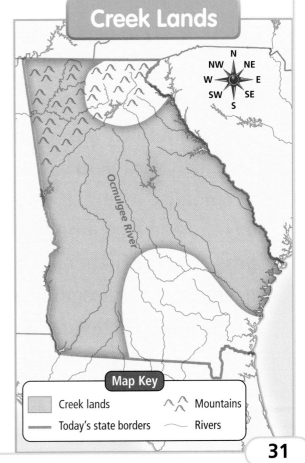

Creek Lands

N
NW NE
W   E
SW SE
S

Ocmulgee River

Map Key

☐ Creek lands
— Today's state borders
⋀⋀ Mountains
〜 Rivers

The Creek played a kind of stick ball game with rackets like these.

Creek Towns

The Creek lived in towns of 400 to 600 people. Around these towns were smaller villages. In the center of a town was an open space called a plaza. Here the Creek held games, weddings, and other ceremonies. A ceremony is a formal act or series of acts done in honor of an event. Near the plaza was a large building that could be used for ceremonies and meetings. One ceremony was the Green Corn Festival. It took place each summer when the corn ripened.

main idea

Houses

The Creek built their houses with things found in nature. For the walls, they covered poles with a mixture of mud and twigs or reeds and tree branches. For the roof, the Creek used bark or bundles of plant stems called thatch. At each end of the roof was an opening to let out the smoke from cooking fires.

Review Where did the Creek hold ceremonies?

The Creek built homes like this one.

Food

The Creek got food by farming, gathering, hunting, and fishing. The Creek women did the farming. They grew corn, squash, pumpkins, beans, and other vegetables. They also gathered wild fruit and nuts. Men fished and hunted for deer and other animals.

main
(★)
idea

Squash, beans, and pumpkins were some of the vegetables the Creek grew in gardens.

milkweed

sassafras tree

cherries

Clothing and Medicines

The Creek used some plants and animals for more than food. They used the skins of the deer for shoes and clothing. From some of the plants, they made teas. From others, they made medicines to treat burns, insect bites, fever, and other problems.

main idea

Review What were some of the things found in nature that the Creek used?

Lesson Review

❶ **Vocabulary** Name two things that you might do on or in a **river.**

❷ **Main Idea** How did the Creek use the natural world around them?

HANDS ON

Activity Draw a plan for a Creek town.

A Creek Town

Long ago, the Creek built their towns in many parts of Georgia. Most towns were built near a river or stream. People used the water for drinking and bathing. Where possible, they traveled on rivers in dugout canoes.

In the towns, each family lived in a group of buildings that included storehouses and summer and winter homes. The buildings stood around a plaza, or open space.

Town leaders met on the plaza. In bad weather, leaders met in the roundhouse.

In this drawing, people use the playing field for target practice. The target is on the top of the tall pole in the middle of the field.

Plaza and playing field

Garden

Roundhouse

Family homes and storehouses

Activities

1. **Describe It** Describe the picture of the Creek town. Use as many details as you can.

2. **Write About It** Tell one thing about life in a Creek town that is like your town and one thing that is different.

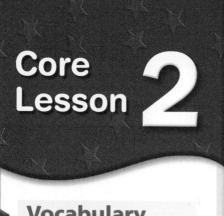

Settlers Come to Georgia

Vocabulary

explorer
colony
settlement
colonist

Reading Skill

Sequence

 STANDARDS

Core
SS2H1a Contributions of James Oglethorpe,
Tomochichi, Mary Musgrove
SS2H1b Everyday life
SSG2b How place impacted settlers

Extend
SS2H1a Contributions of James Oglethorpe,
Tomochichi, Mary Musgrove
SS2CG3 Civility, honesty, dependability

Build on What You Know Have you ever looked all around a new place to find out what it was like?

American Land

Long ago, explorers from Europe came to North America. An **explorer** travels to find new things and places. The explorers hoped to find gold and other riches. They did not find gold, but they did find great forests, wide plains, and many rivers. American Indians already lived there. But kings and queens in Europe wanted the land. They sent people to live in North America.

main idea

English Colonies

A **colony** is a place that is ruled by another country. England was one of the countries that started colonies in North America. People from England traveled in ships to settle the land. Their colonies began with small communities called **settlements.** Two of the earliest settlements were Plymouth and Jamestown. Later, James Oglethorpe (OH guhl thawrp) started Savannah, the first English settlement in what is today Georgia.

main idea

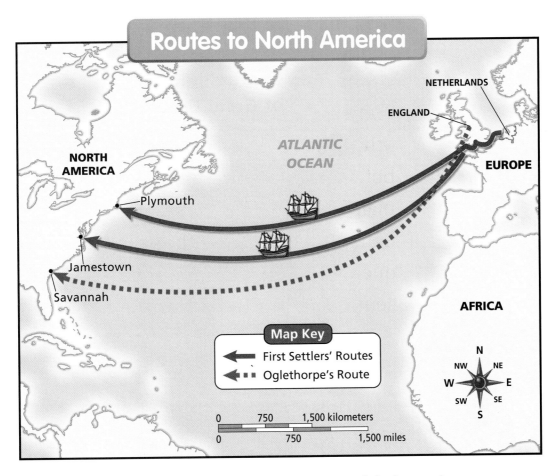

Routes to North America

NETHERLANDS

ENGLAND

NORTH AMERICA

ATLANTIC OCEAN

EUROPE

Plymouth

Jamestown

Savannah

AFRICA

Map Key
⬅ First Settlers' Routes
⬅▪▪▪ Oglethorpe's Route

0   750   1,500 kilometers
0   750   1,500 miles

N
NW   NE
W   E
SW   SE
S

Skill **Reading Maps** Why do you think early settlements were built near water?

Georgia, the Thirteenth Colony

After Jamestown and Plymouth were settled, many more people from England and other parts of Great Britain came to North America. They built colonies up and down the Atlantic coast. Georgia was the thirteenth and last English colony to be settled. James Oglethorpe started the colony more than 100 years after the settling of Plymouth. He named the colony Georgia in honor of the king of Great Britain.

George II, King
of Great Britain

Starting Savannah

In 1733, Oglethorpe brought a group of settlers to Yamacraw (YAHM uh kraw) Bluff on the Savannah River. A bluff is a high place overlooking a river. Oglethorpe chose the high ground because he thought it would be a healthy place for a settlement. The settlement at Yamacraw Bluff became the city of Savannah.

main ★ idea

Savannah was carved out of the great forests of the Georgia colony.

Colonists and the Creek

The leader of the Creek people who lived near Yamacraw Bluff was Tomochichi (TOHM oh chee chee). He made friends with the English colonists. A **colonist** is a person who lives in a colony. The colonists and the Creek traded with each other and treated each other well. The two groups were able to talk to each other with the help of a woman named Mary Musgrove. She spoke both English and Creek.

Mary Musgrove looks on as James Oglethorpe and Tomochichi greet each other.

The artist who made this picture of Savannah drew from his imagination. The background shows mountains where there were none.

James Oglethorpe

James Oglethorpe was a good leader who was so well-liked that the settlers called him Father. A visitor to Savannah said that when people got sick, Oglethorpe would visit them and care for them. The visitor also said that Oglethorpe was able to get people to cheerfully share in the work of building the settlement, even though it was not work they were used to doing. He said, "even the boys and girls do their parts."

main idea ★

Lesson Review

❶ **Vocabulary** Use the words **colony** and **settlement** to tell how the Georgia colony began.

❷ **Main Idea** Explain why James Oglethorpe, Tomochichi, and Mary Musgrove were important to Georgia.

✏ **Activity** Yamacraw Bluff was near the river and it had lots of trees. Write a paragraph to explain why those two things might be important to new settlers.

Early Georgia Heroes

Building a new settlement is hard work. Who would help James Oglethorpe build the Georgia colony?

James Oglethorpe

James Oglethorpe needed the help of many people to make his colony a success. He treated both the American Indians and settlers in Georgia with respect. This civility made him a strong leader.

Oglethorpe made friends with Tomochichi, a leader of a group of Creek called the Yamacraw. His friendship with Tomochichi, and the help of Mary Musgrove, made the new colony grow. Within one year, Oglethorpe had 400 English settlers living in the Georgia colony.

The words on the Oglethorpe family crest mean "He does not know how to give up."

NESCIT CEDERE

This statue of Oglethorpe stands in Savannah, the city he founded.

Mary Musgrove

Mary Musgrove spoke English and some Indian languages. She helped James Oglethorpe and Tomochichi talk to each other. She also helped the settlers and American Indians trade with each other. Musgrove ran a trading post where American Indians brought things such as deerskins or meat. Settlers traded some things they brought from Europe for the deerskins and other things.

Musgrove was dependable. She was always working to settle fights and disagreements between the settlers and American Indians.

Mary Musgrove's Creek name was Coosaponakeesa.

Tomochichi

Tomochichi was the leader of the Yamacraw. He became a friend of James Oglethorpe. Tomochichi agreed to let Oglethorpe start the colony of Georgia on land where the Yamacraw Creek lived. Tomochichi was honest. He kept his promise to Oglethorpe about sharing land with the settlers.

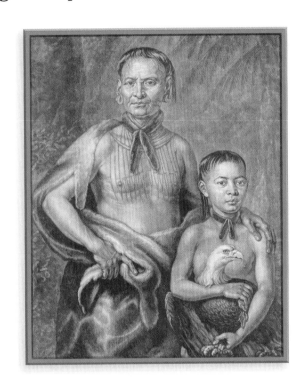

This picture shows Tomochichi with his nephew.

Biographies!

Read more about James Oglethorpe, Mary Musgrove, and Tomochichi.

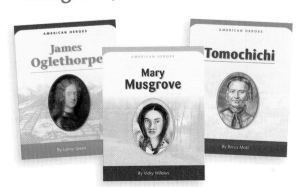

Activities

1. **TALK ABOUT IT** Why do you think these three people worked so well together?

2. **DRAW IT** Make a two-part poster showing ways Tomochichi and Mary Musgrove helped James Oglethorpe start the Georgia colony.

Read a Timeline

▶ **Vocabulary**

timeline

Every family has a history. A timeline can show events in a family's history. A **timeline** is an ordered group of words and dates that shows when events happened.

Look at the timeline of Andrea's family.

Learn the Skill

1930	1940	1950

Step 1 The title tells what the timeline is about. The timeline has a line divided in equal parts. Each part stands for 10 years.

1946
Andrea's grand-father is born.

Step 2 Look at the first and last numbers on the timeline. The numbers are years. The events on the timeline happened between these years.

1935
Andrea's great-grandmother comes to the United States from Japan.

Step 3 The numbers with the events on the timeline tell the year in which each event happened.

Practice the Skill

Use the timeline to answer the questions below.

1 Was Andrea's grandfather born before, or after, her great-grandmother came to the United States?

2 When did Andrea's great-grandmother come to the United States?

3 What happened in 1994?

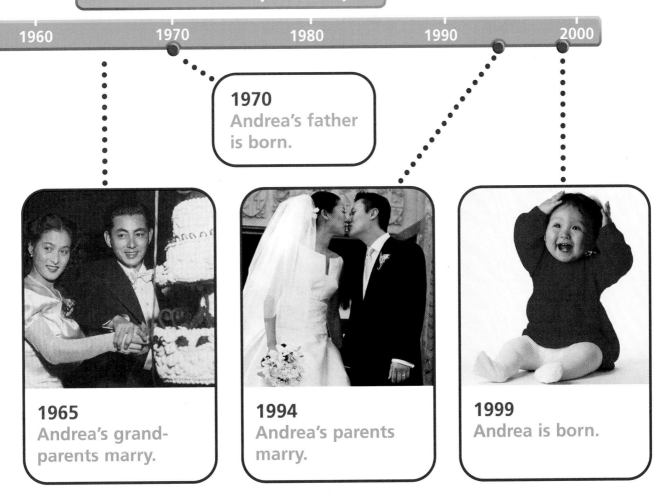

Andrea's Family History

1960   1970   1980   1990   2000

1970
Andrea's father is born.

1965
Andrea's grandparents marry.

1994
Andrea's parents marry.

1999
Andrea is born.

Vocabulary

mountain

valley

Compare and Contrast

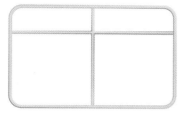

 STANDARDS

Core
SS2H2.a How the Cherokee used resources
SS2G2.b How place impacted the Cherokee

The Cherokee

Build on What You Know

Many people have lived in Georgia before you. Do you think they lived the way you do today?

Life Long Ago

Long ago the Cherokee lived in what is now northern Georgia. All around them were mountains and valleys. A **mountain** is high land with steep sides. Pine forests covered the mountains. A **valley** is low land between mountains. The Cherokee lived in the valleys of the Blue Ridge Mountains.

main idea

Towns

The Cherokee lived in towns with 30 to 60 homes. Like Creek towns, Cherokee towns had an open area for ceremonies and meetings. Each town also had a large, round building for meetings in bad weather. This round building could hold all of the 400 to 500 people of a town.

This map shows where the Cherokee lived in what is now Georgia. They also lived in nearby states.

Cherokee Lands

N NW NE W E SW SE S

Map Key

Cherokee lands

Today's state borders

Mountains

Rivers

The Cherokee grew three main crops of corn, beans, and squash. They were called "the three sisters." The bean plants grew up the cornstalks. The squash plants grew under the beans and the corn.

Town Gardens

Each town also had large fields set aside for gardens. Men and boys helped get the ground ready for planting. Then women and girls planted and tended the crops. The main crops were corn, beans, and squash. Cherokee women also grew other crops such as pumpkins and sunflowers. Men hunted animals and fished for food. The Cherokee got what they needed from the land and water around them.

main ★ idea

Homes

The Cherokee built one home for the cold winters and another home for the hot summers. They used things from nature to make them.

To build summer homes, the Cherokee put wooden posts into the ground. They wove saplings or reeds between the posts to make the walls. They made the roof in almost the same way and covered it with strips of tree bark.

Winter homes were much smaller. They were covered with a thick mix of clay and grass that helped keep the heat in.

Review How did the Cherokee use things from nature?

Sometimes the Cherokee painted the outside walls of a summer home with a paste of ground shells. Winter homes were round and low to the ground.

Other Things from Nature

These pictures show other ways the Cherokee used the things from nature.

Medicines The Cherokee used plants for healing and to help keep people from getting sick. They used different parts of many plants, such as the blackberry, cattail, mint, and sumac. They ground up roots, bark, or stalks. They chewed leaves or boiled them into a tea.

cattails

Baskets Cherokee women made baskets from thin strips of river canes, oak, or maple. They stored food and carried loads in the baskets. Men carried their hunting and fishing tools in baskets too.

Jewelry The Cherokee used shells, animal bones, and copper to make jewelry. They wore it on their fingers, necks, and ears. They also decorated their clothing with porcupine quills and horn and shell rattles.

Review What things did the Cherokee use to make jewelry?

Lesson Review

❶ **Vocabulary** Use the word **valley** in a sentence about where the Cherokee lived.

❷ **Main Idea** How were winter homes different from warm weather homes? How were they alike?

Activity Draw three ways the Cherokee used plants.

A Cherokee Legend

A legend is a story that is told and retold over many, many years. Joseph Bruchac retold this Cherokee legend about **mountains** in Georgia and other southern states.

If we should travel
far to the South,
there in the land
of mountains and mist,
we might hear the story
of how Earth was first shaped.

Water Beetle came out
to see if it was ready,
but the ground was
still as wet as a swamp,
too soft for anyone to stand.

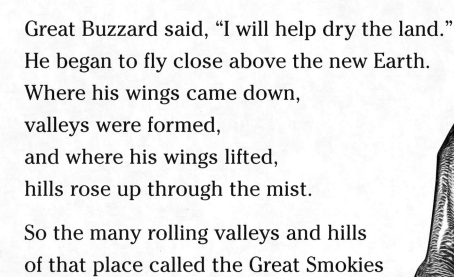

Great Buzzard said, "I will help dry the land."
He began to fly close above the new Earth.
Where his wings came down,
valleys were formed,
and where his wings lifted,
hills rose up through the mist.

So the many rolling valleys and hills
of that place called the Great Smokies
came into being there.

Activities

1. **Talk About It** How does the Cherokee legend say that valleys were formed?

2. **Write About It** Make up a story about how another landform came to be.

Study Artifacts

An **artifact** is an object made in the past. It can be a tool, a bowl, or even something to wear. You can study artifacts to learn more about the people who made them and used them.

► **Vocabulary**

artifact

Learn the Skill

The artifact shown on the next page is a Cherokee bowl. Bowls were made from clay found in ponds near Cherokee villages. Here is how you can find out about this bowl.

Step 1 Think about what you already know. How do you think the Cherokee used the artifact?

Step 2 Study the artifact. What is its shape? Is it shaped like other bowls you have seen?

Step 3 Look at the details. What animal is shown on the bowl?

Practice the Skill

Look at the artifact. Then answer the questions.

1 What are some things the bowl might be used for?

2 Why do you think the Cherokee decorated the bowl with a frog?

3 How is the bowl like bowls in your home? How is it different?

4 If you wanted to decorate a bowl, what would you put on it?

Cherokee bowl

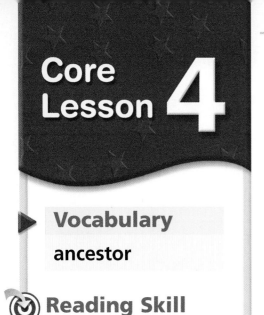

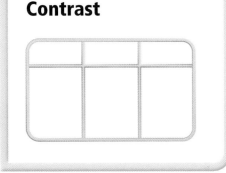

STANDARDS

Core
SS2H2b Compare past Creek and Cherokee cultures
to cultures today
SS2G2d Movement of Creek and Cherokee

Changes in Georgia

Build on What You Know

What can happen when you want to play with a toy that belongs to your sister? White settlers wanted land in Georgia that belonged to American Indians.

Adopting Settlers' Ways

After white settlers came to Georgia, the Cherokee and Creek began to take on some of the settlers' ways. The Cherokee built bigger houses made of logs. Earlier, the Cherokee had shared gardens. Now families had their own farms. They also started raising animals.

This kitchen in a Cherokee home in New Echota looked much like the kitchens in settlers' homes in the 1700s.

The Creek and Cherokee adopted the clothing styles of the settlers. This picture shows John Ross, a Cherokee leader, in about 1836.

Some Creek also built log homes. Others kept the same style of home, but built chimneys instead of leaving smoke holes. They began to use plows to farm. Like the Cherokee, they raised animals. People in both groups began wearing clothing like the settlers wore. The Cherokee made rules and laws to keep order as the settlers had done.

Review What are two ways the coming of white settlers changed Creek and Cherokee life?

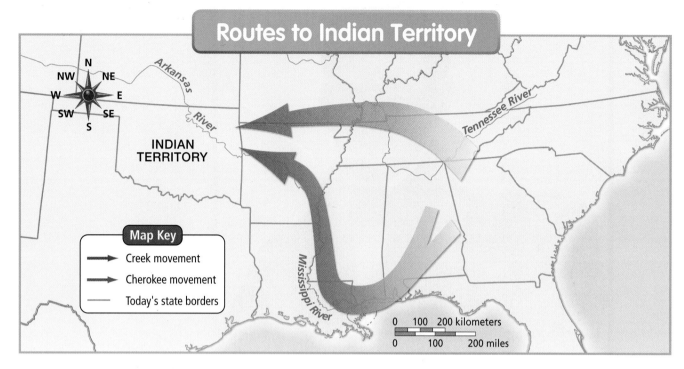

Routes to Indian Territory

INDIAN TERRITORY

Arkansas River

Tennessee River

Mississippi River

N
NW   NE
W   E
SW   SE
S

Map Key
→ Creek movement
→ Cherokee movement
— Today's state borders

0   100   200 kilometers
0   100   200 miles

Many groups of American Indians were forced to move to Indian Territory. Today Indian Territory is the state of Oklahoma.

The Creek Lose Their Lands

As time passed, many more settlers came to Georgia. The Creek had to give up more and more of their lands. Some people went to Florida or Alabama. Others moved to Indian Territory, which is now Oklahoma.

In the 1830s, trouble broke out among different Creek groups in Georgia. United States troops were called in, and a war began. When it was over, the Creek had to give up all their lands. They were forced to move to Indian Territory. Many became sick or died on the long, hard trip.

main
(★)
idea

The Cherokee Trail of Tears

One day gold was found on Cherokee land. Miners came to get the gold. More settlers came too and took Cherokee lands. In 1838, leaders of the United States forced the Cherokee to leave their homes and move to Indian Territory. The United States wanted Cherokee land for miners and settlers. Some Cherokee leaders tried to stop the move, but it did not help. Thousands had to leave their homes. Like the Creek on their journey, many Cherokee became sick, and many others died. This 800-mile trip is known as the Trail of Tears. The Cherokee built new settlements in Oklahoma.

Review Which state is located where Indian Territory was?

On the Trail of Tears, the Cherokee traveled on foot, by boat, and in wagons.

The Cherokee Today

Some Cherokee hid in the mountains and did not go west. They were the ancestors of the Cherokee who live in Georgia today. An **ancestor** is someone in a family who lived in the past. Most Cherokee today live in Oklahoma. They speak English and live in modern homes. They buy their food and clothes in stores. But some still follow the old ways. The Cherokee today keep some of the old ways alive.

main idea

The Cherokee make baskets as their people did in the past.

A mother teaches her child how to sew as Cherokee women have done for many years.

Creek leaders meet in this building in Oklahoma. It is built on a mound to honor the Creek ancestors, who built important buildings on mounds.

The Creek Today

Today, most Creek live in Oklahoma. Most live in the same way that other Americans do. Only a few Creek keep the old ways. They speak the Creek language, and they celebrate the Green Corn Festival. Hardly any Creek stayed in Georgia. Almost all the Creek in Georgia today live in cities or towns and work in many different jobs.

main idea

Review How do most Cherokee and Creek live today?

Lesson Review

❶ **Vocabulary** Use the word **ancestor** in a sentence about the Cherokee or Creek.

❷ **Main Idea** Why, do you think, is the Cherokee journey to Oklahoma called the Trail of Tears?

✎ **Activity** Write a paragraph to tell how the journeys of the Cherokee and Creek were alike.

News from New Echota

New Echota was the capital of the Cherokee's new government. The Cherokee newspaper, the "Cherokee Phoenix," was printed there. One main topic in the paper was the Cherokee fight to stay in their homelands. Most of the Cherokee wanted to stay, but the paper's editor and a few others wanted to give up the fight and move to Indian Territory. This small group signed an agreement giving the United States government all Cherokee lands east of the Mississippi River.

The "Cherokee Phoenix" printed news about the Cherokee government.

Copies of the Cherokee newspaper hang from rafters at the New Echota printshop.

Activities

1. **Talk About It** Why was New Echota an important place to the Cherokee?

2. **Write About It** Why do you think people today visit places, such as New Echota, that were important in the past?

Use a Grid

Grids can help you find places and things on many kinds of maps. A **grid** is a pattern of lines. The lines make columns and rows. Each column has a letter, and each row has a number. The letters and the numbers name each square.

▶ **Vocabulary**

grid
location

Learn the Skill

Step 1 Look at this grid. Put your finger on the star. Move it straight up to the top of the column. What is the letter?

Step 2 Put your finger on the star again. Move it sideways to the beginning of the row. What is the number?

Step 3 Together, the letter and number name the square. The name of the square with the star is B3. That is the place, or **location,** where the star can be found.

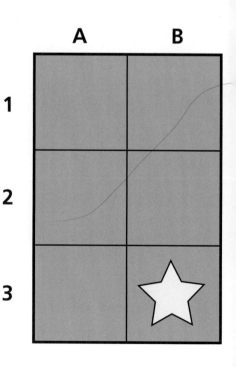

Practice the Skill

Look at the map. Then answer the questions.

1 Where is the library located? Name the square.

2 Where is the post office located? Name the square.

3 What is located in square D4?

Big Ideas

Timeline in Georgia History

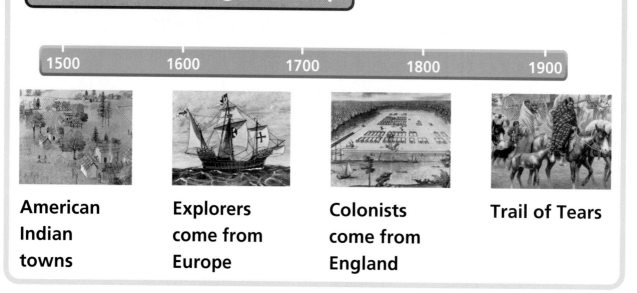

| 1500 | 1600 | 1700 | 1800 | 1900 |

American Indian towns

Explorers come from Europe

Colonists come from England

Trail of Tears

Find the missing words on the timeline.

1. _____ were living in America before explorers came.
2. _____ came after explorers from Europe.
3. The 1830s journey that the Cherokee were forced to make is called the _____ .

Facts and Main Ideas

4. What are some ways the Creek used rivers? (page 31)

5. Why did James Oglethorpe choose Yamacraw Bluff as a place for the Savannah settlement? (page 41)

6. What are two kinds of homes that the Cherokee built? (page 53)

7. Why were the Creek and Cherokee forced to leave Georgia? (pages 62, 63)

Vocabulary

Choose the letter of the correct word.

8. Someone in a family who lived in the past

9. Lowland between mountains

10. A large body of moving water that flows into another body of water

11. A person who travels to find new things and places

12. A place ruled by another country

A. **river** (page 31)

B. **explorer** (page 38)

C. **colony** (page 39)

D. **colonist** (page 42)

E. **valley** (page 50)

F. **ancestor** (page 64)

 Test Practice

13. What does the word **history** mean?

   A. a long trip
   B. a Savannah colonist
   C. everything you can know about the past
   D. a place ruled by another country

Critical Thinking

Compare

14. How did James Oglethorpe, Tomochichi, and Mary Musgrove help the colony of Georgia?

Review and Test Prep

Read a Timeline

Dan's Life History

0 1 2 3 4 5 6 7 8 9

Dan was born

Dan learned to read

Dan today

15. How old is Dan today?

16. What did Dan do when he was six?

Use a Grid

17. Where is the cafeteria? Use the grid to name the square.

18. What is in square 4B?

Brown Elementary School

	1	2	3	4
A		Principal's office		
B		Cafeteria		Library
C			Gymnasium	

Connect to Georgia

Unit Activity

Make a History Puppet

Choose a person from Georgia history and make a puppet of that person.

❶ Make the puppet's head and costume.

❷ Write three questions that you would like people to ask your puppet.

❸ Use your hand and voice so that your puppet answers the questions.

CURRENT EVENTS
WEEKLY (WR) READER

Current Events Project

What events are taking place in your area? Make an **Events in the News Timeline.**

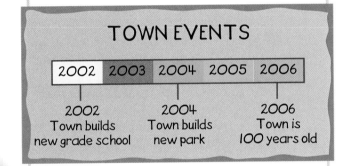

TOWN EVENTS

2002	2003	2004	2005	2006

2002
Town builds new grade school

2004
Town builds new park

2006
Town is 100 years old

Technology

Read articles about current events at **www.eduplace.com/kids/hmss/**

Personal Finance

Cherokee men and women did different jobs to get food. Today men and women do most of the same jobs. Make a list of jobs people do to get or make food.

American Heroes
Read About It

Look for these biographies in your classroom.

UNIT 2

Georgia's Places

"Wherever life takes us, there are always moments of wonder."

—Jimmy Carter, President, 1977–1981

The Big Idea

Why is the world around you important in your life?

Unit 2 Georgia's Places

Vocabulary Preview

Technology

e • glossary
e • word games
www.eduplace.com/kids/hmss/

continent

The United States is on the continent of North America. A **continent** is a large body of land. page 80

climate

Climate is the usual weather of a place over a long time. People in a cold climate need warm homes to live in. page 87

Reading Strategy

Use the **question** reading strategy in Lessons 1, 2, and 3 and the **monitor and clarify** strategy in Lessons 4 and 5.

landform

A **landform** is one of the shapes of land found on the earth. One kind of landform is a mountain.

page 94

natural resource

Water is an important natural resource. A **natural resource** is something in nature that people use. page 104

Where You Live

Vocabulary

nation
state
continent

Reading Skill

Classify

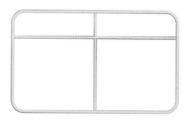

STANDARDS

Core
Geographic Understandings
GPS Map and Globe Skill 6: information from maps

Extend
GPS Map and Globe Skill 1: cardinal directions

Build on What You Know

What do you call the community where you live? Do you know the rest of your address?

States in a Country

Carlos is going to mail a letter to his cousin Len. Len lives on Green Street in the city of Columbus. Carlos has written that address on the envelope.

return address

stamp

Carlos Rivera
95 Rock Street
Toronto, Ontario
Canada
M6C 2J9

Len Ruis
27 Green Street
Columbus, Georgia 31
U.S.A.

address

Carlos

The United States of America

Map Key
• City

Toronto

Columbus

The city of Columbus is in the state of Georgia.

The letters U.S.A. on the envelope stand for the nation called the United States of America. A **nation** is a land where people have the same laws and leaders. Another word for **nation** is **country.** Georgia is a state in the United States. A **state** is a part of a nation. The United States is a nation made up of 50 states.

Len

main ★ idea

Review Which state is west of Georgia?

Continents

If you were an astronaut looking at the earth from a space station, you would see mostly oceans. You would also see some very large bodies of land. Most of those large bodies of land are **continents.** (★) main idea

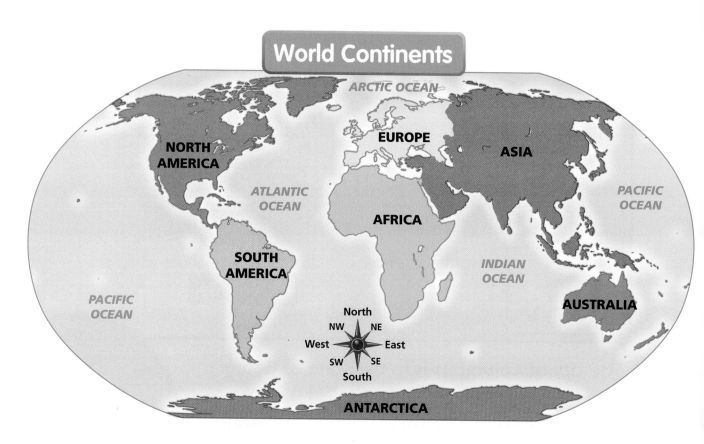

World Continents

ARCTIC OCEAN

NORTH AMERICA

EUROPE

ASIA

ATLANTIC OCEAN

PACIFIC OCEAN

AFRICA

SOUTH AMERICA

INDIAN OCEAN

PACIFIC OCEAN

AUSTRALIA

North

NW NE

West — East

SW SE

South

ANTARCTICA

Skill **Reading Maps** Find and name the seven continents on the map. Find and name the four oceans.

North America

The United States is on the continent of North America. The United States shares North America with two other large nations. They are Canada and Mexico. Seven small nations south of Mexico and many island nations are part of North America too.

Which oceans touch North America?

Review What is one way that Mexico and the United States are alike?

Lesson Review

1 **Vocabulary** Write a sentence that tells where you live. Use the words **nation**, **state**, and **continent** in the sentence.

2 **Main Idea** What are the earth's seven continents?

Activity Draw an envelope for a letter to a friend. Write your address and your friend's address on it.

Finding Your Way

How have people found their way when sailing across the oceans? A magnetic compass helped many sailors.

A magnetic compass is like a compass rose. It shows directions: north, south, east, and west. But a magnetic compass has something more. It has a needle that is a magnet. Because the needle is a magnet, it always points toward the north. Once you know where north is, you can find east, south, and west too.

People in China were the first to make magnetic compasses.

Read a Magnetic Compass

① Rest the compass on a table. Find the colored end of the needle. That end points north.

② Locate the letters N, E, S, and W. Name the direction word that each letter stands for.

③ Gently turn the compass until the needle is in line with the letter N. What does the needle do when you turn the compass?

④ Hold both arms out together ahead of you and face the direction that the compass points. You should be facing and pointing north.

Use Intermediate Directions

▶ **Vocabulary**

intermediate directions

When people travel from one city to another they often use maps to find their way. A compass rose shows them the map directions.

Learn the Skill

Look at the compass rose below.

Step 1 Find the letters N, S, E, and W. They stand for the main direction words: north, south, east, and west.

Step 2 Find the line halfway between north and east. This line is labeled NE because it points in the direction called northeast.

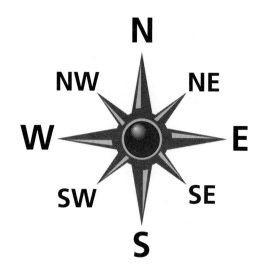

Step 3 Now find the other halfway lines. What do their labels stand for? These directions are called **intermediate directions.**

Practice the Skill

Look at the map. Then follow the directions.

1 Find Gettysburg, Pennsylvania. In what direction do you go to get to Selma, Alabama?

2 Find St. Paul, Minnesota. What direction do you go to get to Macon, Georgia?

3 Leave Santa Fe, New Mexico, and travel northeast. Which city on this map do you reach first?

United States

Weather and Climate

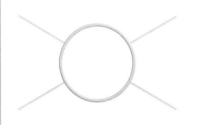
Build on What You Know

Is it raining or sunny today? What it is like outside makes a difference in the activities you do each day.

Weather

Weather is what the air is like outside at any given time. People often want to know about weather because it affects their lives. Scientists measure weather in many ways. They also try to predict weather. Here is a weather report.

main idea

Today		Tomorrow	
	Sunny, warm 65° – 70°F		Cloudy 60° – 62°F
	Winds up to 10 miles an hour		Chance of rain

Skill Chart Reading What do the words, numbers, and pictures tell about weather?

Climate

Climate is the usual weather of a place over a long time. A climate can have different kinds of weather. Jim and Jenna tell about the climate where they live.

main idea

July can be very hot in Milwaukee, Wisconsin.

Jim

January can be really cold.

Jim

Lithia Springs, Georgia, has warm weather most of the year.

Jenna

Rain storms are part of our climate too.

Jenna

Review What are two kinds of weather that could be in one climate?

Living in Different Climates

Climates make a difference in the way people live. main idea

In what ways are these two climates different?

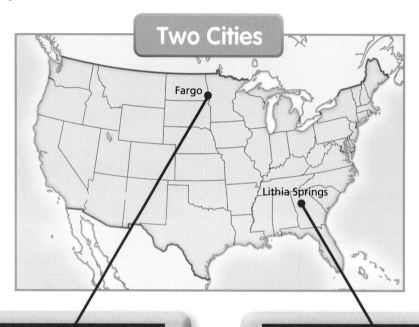

Two Cities

Fargo

Lithia Springs

Fargo, North Dakota, has a climate that is very cold in winter.

People need:
- warm air in buildings and cars in winter
- clothes to keep out snow and cold

Lithia Springs, Georgia, has a climate that is hot in summer. Snow is very rare.

People need:
- cool air in buildings and cars much of the year
- light clothes to wear

Cold Climate Job

How do you know that this picture was not taken in Lithia Springs, Georgia?

Farmers raise plants and animals that do well in their climate. Builders think of climate when they plan homes and other buildings. Also, some jobs fit one climate and not another. Driving a snowplow is one example. Mostly, though, people have found ways to live in almost all climates.

Review What is one way that climate makes a difference in what people do?

Lesson Review

❶ **Vocabulary** Write sentences to explain the difference between **weather** and **climate.**

❷ **Main Idea** Explain how weather and climate are related.

HANDS ON **Activity** Draw a picture that shows how climate affects people where you live. Explain your drawing.

The Young Woman and the Thunder Beings

People all over the world have told stories to explain the natural world. Joseph Bruchac retells this Seneca legend about thunderstorms in **Between Earth and Sky.**

To the North lived the Longhouse People, near the edge of the falls called Ne-ah-ga.

They sometimes spoke of the Thunder Beings who lived in a cave beneath the falls. When a child wanted to give thanks to the Thunderers for the gift of rain, he would place an offering in a canoe and put it in the river to float over the falls.

One day a young woman alone in her canoe was crossing the river far up from the falls when she lost her paddle. The current was swift and she found herself swept away. This brave young woman had always been a friend of the Thunderers, giving them gifts with each new season. So, as she fell, she did not scream or cry. In trust, she asked calmly for help.

The Thunder Beings saved her life, catching her safely in their blanket. Then the chief of the Thunderers asked the young woman to be his wife. She agreed, and to this day, the Seneca say that when the rumbling voices of the Thunder Beings roll across the sky, the brave young woman is keeping watch, reminding us that every gift we give gives us back a blessing.

Activities

1. **Talk About It** Why did the Thunder Beings save the girl?

2. **Act It Out** List the characters in the story and act out what they do.

Georgia's Regions

Vocabulary

region
landform
coast
plateau
ridge

Reading Skill

Compare and Contrast

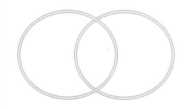

Wind has made ripples in the sand on one of Georgia's many islands.

 STANDARDS

Core
SS2G1a Georgia's geographic regions

Extend
SS2H1a Sequoyah (development of
  Cherokee alphabet)
SSCG3 Patience

Build on What You Know

Have you traveled to another part of Georgia? If you drive across Georgia, you will see that the land is not the same in all parts of the state.

Looking at Georgia

Georgia has five main regions. A **region** is an area that has some shared feature. Georgia's regions have different landforms. A **landform** is one of the shapes of land found on the earth. A mountain is one kind of landform. The map on page 95 shows where Georgia's regions are.

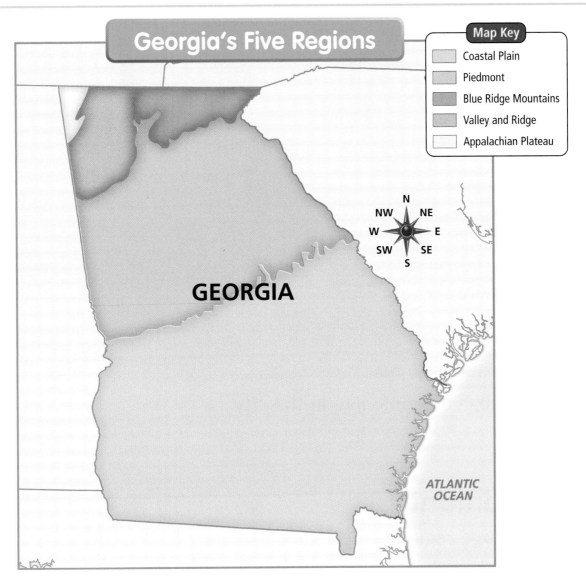

Georgia's Five Regions

Map Key
- Coastal Plain
- Piedmont
- Blue Ridge Mountains
- Valley and Ridge
- Appalachian Plateau

GEORGIA

ATLANTIC OCEAN

Skill In what part of the state is the Coastal Plain?

The Coastal Plain

The largest region in Georgia is the Coastal Plain. This is flat or nearly flat land along the coast. A **coast** is land next to a sea or an ocean. Pine and oak trees grow in the sandy soil of this region. Farmers grow pecans and peanuts here.

Review What is the largest region in Georgia?

More than 400,000 people live in the city of Atlanta.

The Piedmont

Another large region of Georgia is called the Piedmont (PEED mahnt). The land here is hilly with many forests. Wood from the trees in these forests is used to make boxes, barrels, and other things.

Most of Georgia's people live in the Piedmont. Seven of the state's ten largest cities are in this region. These cities are Atlanta, Augusta, Columbus, Athens, Macon, Roswell, and Marietta.

Appalachian Plateau

The Appalachian Plateau (ap uh LAY chee uhn pla TOH) takes up a small corner of northwestern Georgia. A **plateau** is an area of fairly flat high land. The area also has mountains. Two of them are Sand Mountain and Lookout Mountain. The temperatures in this northern region are lower than in the southern part of the state. People build vacation homes here to enjoy the cool weather of the high lands during hot summer months.

Review In what part of Georgia do most people live?

Cloudland Canyon State Park is in the Appalachian Plateau region.

Valley and Ridge

In the north of Georgia is the Valley and Ridge region. A **ridge** is a long, narrow strip of high land. Many of the ridges in this region are rocky and covered with forests. But the soil in the valleys is good for farming. People grow fruits such as apples here. People go hiking and camping in this region too.

This farm is in a valley in the Valley and Ridge region.

The highest point in Georgia is Brasstown Bald Mountain.

Blue Ridge Mountains

The Blue Ridge Mountains region is in the northeastern part of the state. These mountains are the southernmost part of the Appalachian Mountains. Georgia's highest mountains are here. Some of the state's big rivers begin in these mountains. The rushing waters of the rivers provide power to make electricity.

Review What are three regions in the northernmost part of Georgia?

Lesson Review

1 **Vocabulary** Tell about two of Georgia's regions using the words **plateau** and **coast.**

2 **Main Idea** Compare the Piedmont region with the Coastal Plain. How are these regions alike and different?

Activity Make a list of the regions. Next to each region write one fact about that region.

Sequoyah

Sequoyah was a Cherokee who gave his people a great gift. He invented an alphabet. Like other American Indians, the Cherokee shared news and stories by talking to one another. They had no way of writing their language. Sequoyah saw that Georgia settlers could read and write in English. He wanted the Cherokee to read and write in their language, too.

Sequoyah worked on his alphabet for years while living in northeastern Georgia. When he finally finished it, his patience had paid off. Soon most Cherokee were reading and writing in their own language.

This traffic sign is written in both Cherokee and English.

Sequoyah's alphabet was called "talking leaves." It now has 85 letters.

Biographies!
Read more about Sequoyah.

Activities

1. **TALK ABOUT IT** Compare the alphabet in the picture above to the English alphabet you use.

2. **WRITE ABOUT IT** Why do you think it is useful for people to learn to read and write?

Skillbuilder

Identify Main Idea and Details

▶ **Vocabulary**

main idea
detail

Knowing about main ideas and details can help you understand what you read.

Learn the Skill

Look for the **main idea** and **details** in this paragraph.

> Different kinds of trees grow in different regions of the United States. Honey mesquite (meh SKEET) trees grow where it is hot and dry. White spruce trees grow where it is cold in winter. Live oak trees grow in warm, wet regions.

(★) *main idea*

Live oak leaves and acorns

Step 1 The main idea tells what the whole paragraph is about. In this paragraph, the first sentence tells the main idea. But the main idea can be any sentence that tells what the whole paragraph is about.

Step 2 The other sentences in this paragraph give the details. Each detail tells more about the main idea.

Practice the Skill

Read the paragraph below and look at the map.

1 Tell the main idea of this paragraph.

2 Give one detail from the paragraph and one detail from the map that tell more about the main idea.

Some regions of the United States get more rain than others. It rains the most on the northwest coast of the United States. The southeast region gets a lot of rain too. The region that gets the least rain is the southwest.

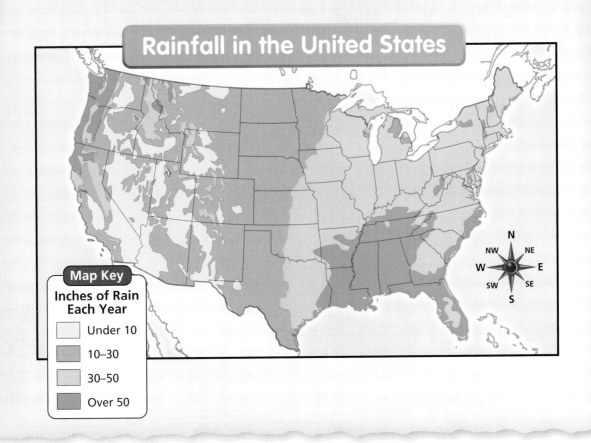

Rainfall in the United States

Map Key
Inches of Rain Each Year

Under 10
10–30
30–50
Over 50

Vocabulary

natural resource

environment

 Reading Skill

Sequence

STANDARDS

Core
SS2H2a Georgia resources

Extend
SS2G1b Georgia's rivers

Georgia's Resources

Build on What You Know

Do you have plants in your classroom? What do plants need to grow? Most plants need air, soil, water, and sunlight. These things are all found in nature. People did not make them.

Natural Resources

Like plants, people use things from nature. Something in nature that people use is called a **natural resource.** Air, soil, and water are natural resources. Trees, rocks, and oil are too.

This drawing shows that peanuts grow underground. Georgia produces more peanuts than any other state in the United States.

Resources for Farming

People in Georgia have many resources to use and enjoy. For Georgia's farmers, an important resource is the state's climate. Georgia stays warm for much of the year, and it has plenty of rain. During the long growing season, farmers grow peanuts, pecans, peaches, cotton, and many other crops.

main idea

Review Why is climate an important resource for Georgia's farmers?

Resources in the Ground

Some of Georgia's resources are in the ground. The state produces large amounts of clay. Georgia leads the states in producing a kind of clay called kaolin (KAY uh lihn). Kaolin is used in making pots and in making a glossy finish on paper. Georgians also get sand, gravel, and stone from the ground. Georgia produces marble and granite. Marble and granite are kinds of stone used in building.

The statue of Abraham Lincoln in Washington, D.C., is made from Georgia marble.

Other Georgia Resources

Georgia has many other resources. People use the forests and rivers and lakes for camping and swimming and boating. People make paper from the state's trees. Ships can carry many things on some of the rivers. Dams on some rivers help in making electricity. The lakes that form behind the dams provide water for homes and businesses to use.

Review What are two ways people use Georgia's waterways?

Large ships can travel on the Savannah River between Savannah and the Atlantic Ocean.

main idea

cargo ship

tug boat

barge

Savannah River

People and the Land

The natural world around you is called the **environment.** Land, water, plants, animals, and people are all part of the environment. Everything people do to the environment has an effect.

For example, plants are an important part of our environment. The roots of trees and other plants help hold the soil down. If you cut down trees, the soil may blow away in the wind. Rain may wash away soil. Losing soil is an effect of people's actions.

People have planted trees to replace some of the ones they cut down.

People recycle paper, plastic, and metals to save resources.

In the past, people did many things to hurt the environment. Some countries made laws to protect the environment. People had to start to clean up the land and water. They had to find ways to keep the air and water clean. Because of the laws and people's actions, some parts of our environment are cleaner than they used to be.

Lesson Review

❶ **Vocabulary** Write a sentence describing the **environment** around your home or school.

❷ **Main Idea** Name three Georgia resources and explain how you use them.

Activity Write or tell about something that you can do to help take care of the environment.

Geography

Georgia's Rivers

What has two banks but no money? (Answer: a river) Georgia is a state of many rivers.

People use river water for drinking, for work, and for play. Long ago, American Indians lived along these rivers. Later, settlers from Europe followed the rivers and built towns on the river banks. Farmers brought their cotton to ships that carried it on the rivers to the coast.

Today, people in Georgia still use the rivers for work and play.

Georgia's Rivers

Map Key

— State border

〜 Rivers

Many of Georgia's rivers flow into the Atlantic Ocean. Trace the routes of the Altamaha and St. Mary's rivers.

Tugboats pull heavy loads on the Savannah River.

Activities

1. **TALK ABOUT IT** Look at the pictures. How do people use rivers?

2. **LIST IT** Use the map above or the Atlas map on page R21 to make a list of Georgia's rivers.

Vocabulary

transportation
invention
communication

Reading Skill

Cause and Effect

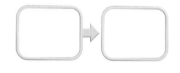

STANDARDS

Core
SS2H1b Everyday life past and present

Georgia Changes

Build on What You Know Has your school bought any new equipment for the playground or classrooms? Did that change how students work and play?

Sailing to Georgia

James Oglethorpe and his group of English settlers used sailing ships for their transportation to North America. Their trip across the Atlantic Ocean took two months. **Transportation** is any way of moving things or people from one place to another. Today, the trip by air from England to Georgia takes only about eight hours.

main idea

Mail, packages, food, and other things are sent around the country and the world by air.

Transportation Changes

In Georgia's early days, people traveled on land from place to place by foot or horseback. In some places, they could use a horse-drawn wagon. Today new kinds of transportation have changed how people live. People in Georgia can get from place to place more quickly and easily using cars, trucks, buses, trains, or airplanes. Businesses can send people and things more quickly too.

Review In what ways have airplanes changed how people in Georgia live?

Communication Changes

Trains, cars, and airplanes are only a few of the inventions that have changed our lives. An **invention** is something new that someone makes or thinks of.

In Mary Musgrove's time, people wrote letters on paper. The letters were carried by people walking or riding horseback. Today we have many new inventions that have made communication much faster than sending letters. **Communication** is any way of sharing news. Radios, TVs, and computers allow instant communication today.

(★) main idea

The first telephones were very different from today's cell phones.

Then

The dishwasher is an invention that makes housework easier.

Now

Inventions Change Our Lives

Look around your home, school, and community. You will see many things that people of Tomochichi's time could not have imagined. <u>These new inventions save time and make many kinds of work easier.</u>

main idea

Review What is one way we communicate today?

Lesson Review

❶ **Vocabulary** Describe a form of **communication** that you use.

❷ **Cause and Effect** Choose an invention and explain how it has changed life in your community.

HANDS ON

Activity Make a mural to show how people traveled in the past and how they travel today.

Extend
Lesson 5
History

Inventions and Change

A Cool Timeline

For hundreds of years, people have found ways to keep food from spoiling by keeping it cold. There were many ways to keep food cold before people used refrigerators. Look at how the ways have changed.

1750 ⸱⸱⸱⸱⸱⸱ **1800**

250 years ago
Settlers dug root cellars inside or outside their homes.

Keeping Food Cold

1850　　　　　1900　　　　　1950　　　　　2000

170 years ago
A big block of ice kept food inside the ice box cold. The iceman delivered a new block of ice every other day or so.

80 years ago
People began using electric refrigerators with freezers.

Activities

1. **Figure It Out** About how many years apart are the ice box and the electric refrigerator?

2. **Talk About It** Tell a story about a time when the electricity was out and your family could not keep food cold in the refrigerator.

Study Skills

Skillbuilder

Identify Primary and Secondary Sources

▶ **Vocabulary**

primary
source

secondary
source

Many people have written or spoken about their lives. Their stories are primary sources. A **primary source** is information from a person who was there. A primary source can be an artifact, a photograph, a letter, a notebook, or many other things. Primary sources are different from secondary sources. A **secondary source** is information written by a person who was not there.

Read the two passages below. One is a primary source. The other is a secondary source.

> **A** "I then shouted into [the mouthpiece] the following sentence: 'Mr. Watson—come here—I want to see you.' To my delight he came and declared that he had heard and understood what I said."
> – From the notebook of Alexander Graham Bell, 1876

> **B** Alexander Graham Bell worked on his telephone invention for years. Finally, on March 10, 1876, he made it work. Bell spoke into his telephone and his assistant, Thomas Watson, was able to hear his words.
> – From an encyclopedia article

Learn the Skill

Step 1 Read the A and B sources carefully. What are they about?

Step 2 As you read, look for clues. A primary source may have *I, me,* or *we.*

Step 3 If the information tells what the writer heard or read about the event, it is a secondary source. What words tell you that someone is reporting what he or she heard or read about?

Practice the Skill

Answer these questions.

1 How are sources A and B alike?

2 Which is the primary source? Explain your answer.

3 Which is the secondary source? Explain your answer.

This page comes from the notebook of Alexander Graham Bell. The notebook is a primary source.

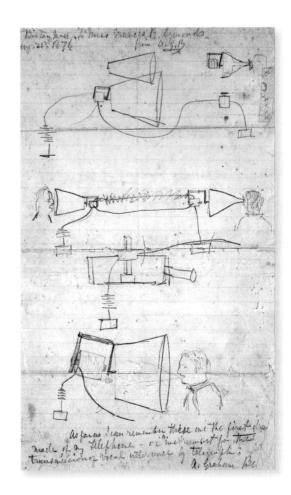

Unit 2 Review and Test Prep

Big Ideas

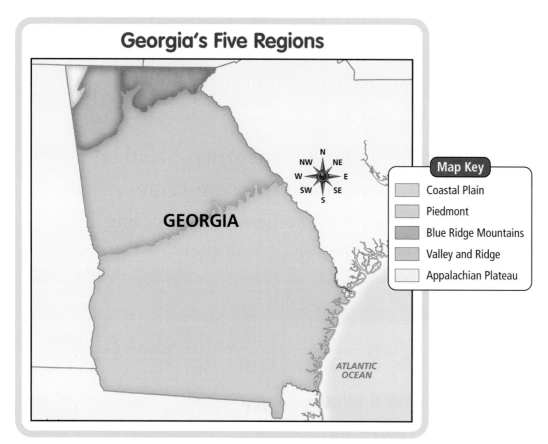

Georgia's Five Regions

Map Key

- Coastal Plain
- Piedmont
- Blue Ridge Mountains
- Valley and Ridge
- Appalachian Plateau

GEORGIA

ATLANTIC OCEAN

Use the map to help you fill in the blanks.

1. The largest region in Georgia is the _____. 2. North of that region is the _____. 3. The three smaller regions are, from west to east, the _____, the _____, and the _____. 4. To the east of the largest region is a large body of water called the _____.

Facts and Main Ideas

5. How are weather and climate related? (pages 86, 87)

6. What gift did Sequoyah give the Cherokee? (page 100)

7. Name three of Georgia's natural resources. (pages 105–107)

Vocabulary

Choose the missing word in each sentence.

8. A _____ is an area of fairly high flat land.

9. A country may also be called a _____.

10. The _____ is the natural world around us.

11. A _____ is a long, narrow strip of high land.

A. **nation** (page 79)

B. **region** (page 94)

C. **plateau** (page 97)

D. **ridge** (page 98)

E. **environment** (page 108)

 Test Practice

12. What do the words **natural resource** mean?

   A. something that people make

   B. something in nature that people use

   C. a place where people cannot live

   D. something that people invented

Critical Thinking

Cause and Effect

13. Explain the effect of new transportation inventions on the way people live.

14. Explain the effect of new communication inventions on the way people live.

Review and Test Prep

Skillbuilders   Use Intermediate Directions

15. In which direction do you go to get from Phoenix, Arizona, to Carson City, Nevada?

16. If you go southeast from Salt Lake City, which city do you reach?

Identify Main Idea and Details

The huge Okefenokee Swamp is home for many reptiles. Alligators share the swamp waters with other reptiles, including snakes. Some of the snakes are harmless. Others are dangerous. Copperheads, corals, and water moccasins are poisonous snakes that live in the swamp. It is also home to many birds and other kinds of animals.

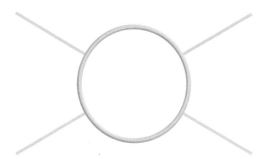

17. Copy the web on a sheet of paper. In the circle, write the main idea of the paragraph above. Put details on the lines.

Connect to Georgia

Unit Activity

Keep a Weather Log

Keep track of the weather for a week and make a weather log.

❶ Record the temperature each day.

❷ Note whether it is cloudy, sunny, or raining.

❸ Make a weather map for one day to go with your log.

Current Events Project

Find information about places in your region. Make a **Landform Map.**

Blue Ridge Mountains

Technology

Read articles about current events at www.eduplace.com/kids/hmss/

Personal Finance

Name something that a person in a warm climate like Georgia's might choose to buy that a person in a cold climate would not.

American Heroes
Read About It

Look for this biography in your classroom.

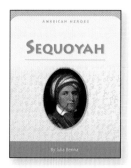

AMERICAN HEROES

SEQUOYAH

By Julia Benna

UNIT 3

Georgia at Work

"There is no substitute for hard work."

—Thomas Edison, inventor

The Big Idea

What are ways people earn, spend, and save money?

Unit 3 Georgia at Work

Vocabulary Preview

Technology

e • **glossary**
e • **word games**
www.eduplace.com/kids/hmss/

producer

A **producer** is someone who provides a service or makes goods. This worker builds cars, so he is a producer. page 132

consumer

A **consumer** is someone who buys goods or services. You are a consumer when you buy fruits and vegetables. page 132

Reading Strategy

Use the **question** reading strategy in Lessons 1 and 2 and the **summarize** strategy in Lessons 3 and 4.

income

The money people earn when they work is their **income.** Sam's income is the $5.00 he earns each week on his paper route.

page 134

price

Price is the amount of money you pay to buy something. If you look in two or three stores, you may find the same toy at different prices. **page 150**

Vocabulary

needs
shelter
wants
opportunity cost
benefit

Reading Skill
Cause and Effect

Needs, Wants, and Choices

Build on What You Know

Have you bought anything at a store? What choices did you make?

Needs and Wants

Needs are things that people must have to live. Everyone has to have food, water, clothing, and shelter. **Shelter** is something that protects or covers. Houses, trailer homes, and apartments are kinds of shelter.

Wants are things that people would like to have. People do not have to have those things to live. Everyone has wants and needs.

main idea

Houses in the northern United States give shelter from snow.

 **STANDARDS**

Core
SS2E1 Choices and opportunity costs
SS2E4 Costs and benefits

Making Choices

People cannot have everything they want. People have to make choices. What they give up is called the **opportunity cost.** What they get is the **benefit.**

I have $30 saved. I can buy a computer game and play with it today. Or I can buy a scooter and ride it in the spring.

Sally's Choices

Choices	What I Give Up (Opportunity Cost)	What I Get (Benefit)
Buy computer game	Ride scooter in spring	Enjoy computer game today
Buy scooter	Enjoy computer game today	Ride scooter in spring

Review If Sally buys the computer game, what does she give up?

Lesson Review

❶ **Vocabulary** Name some **needs** and some **wants.**

❷ **Main Idea** What is the opportunity cost of buying the scooter?

✎ **Activity** List as many kinds of shelter as you can.

Extend Lesson 1
Literature

THE MILKMAID

"The Milkmaid" is a tale told in Mexico and many other countries.

❖ ❖ ❖

Maria was a milkmaid who worked for a rich family. Sometimes the family gave Maria their leftover milk. Maria made extra money by selling the milk. One day the family gave Maria enough milk to fill a big jug.

On her way to market to sell the milk she thought, "I will have money to buy a hen that will lay many eggs. I will sell the eggs and use the money to buy a pig."

"When the pig has grown large, I will sell it and buy a cow. My cow will always give me milk to sell."

Maria thought of all the money she would make, and skipped with joy. Then, oops! Down she fell! Crash went the milk jug! Out spilled the milk, and with it Maria's dreams.

Maria cried and cried. Finally she said, "I may not get all I wanted, but I still have what I need."

Activities

1. **Write About It** Make a list of all of Maria's wants.

2. **Think About It** When Maria says, "I still have what I need," what are some needs she may be thinking of?

People at Work

Vocabulary
producer
consumer
income

Reading Skill
Draw Conclusions

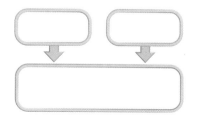

Build on What You Know
Do you make the things you need and want? Do you buy them?

Getting Things We Need

Hungry? Want an apple to eat? If you are the farmer who grows the apple, you are a **producer.** A producer is a person who makes or grows something. If you are the person who buys the apple and eats it, you are a **consumer.** A consumer is someone who buys or uses things.

What if you grow the apple and eat the apple? Then you are a producer and a consumer.

main idea

STANDARDS

Core
SS2E3 Use money to get goods, services

Extend
SS2H1a Contributions of Jackie Robinson
SS2CG3 Character traits: good sportsmanship

Ways to Earn Money

When people work, they usually earn money. This money is their **income.**

One person's income may be earned from selling a painting he made. Another person may earn money by selling a crop she grew. Sometimes people sell their skills or their time. They are paid for teaching in a school or working in a shop. People do different kinds of work.

main idea

I own a small business. I like to help people with computer problems. I also like being my own boss!

I run this machine. I am really good at making cars.

I work all day. At night, I go to school. I want to be a chef and make really tasty meals for people!

I like to make people's homes look beautiful.

Review What work do people do to earn money?

Lesson Review

1 **Vocabulary** Name two ways to earn **income**.

2 **Main Idea** What is a way that someone can be both a producer and a consumer?

HANDS ON **Activity** Draw a picture that shows a job you might like to do someday.

Jackie Robinson

Some people might say that Jackie Robinson had one of the hardest jobs in the world. He was a star baseball player, but playing baseball was not the hard part.

In 1947, Robinson became the first African American player on a major league team. Some white people did not want him on the team. They did hurtful things to make him quit. But he did not quit. Instead of showing anger, he showed good sportsmanship. People looked up to Robinson because of his talent and his good sportsmanship.

Robinson said,

"I'm not concerned with your liking or disliking me. . . . All I ask is that you respect me as a human being."

A Georgia Hero

Jackie Robinson helped his team, the Brooklyn Dodgers, become champs.

Biographies!
Read more about Jackie Robinson.

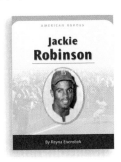

Activities

1. **TALK ABOUT IT** In what way does the picture above show Robinson's talent?

2. **WRITE ABOUT IT** Look at the picture above. Write a headline for a news article to go with it.

Use a Map Scale

The things that people make need to be moved from place to place. A map scale can tell you how far they go.

▶ **Vocabulary**

distance
scale

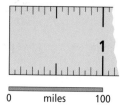

1

0   miles   100

Learn the Skill

Distance is how far one point is from another. You can use a map and a map **scale** to figure out distance. A map scale is a symbol on a map that can help you measure distances.

Step 1 Look at the map scale and the ruler. The blue scale bar measures one inch.

Step 2 Look at the numbers on the scale. They show that one inch on the map stands for 100 miles. How many miles do two inches stand for?

Step 3 It is about five inches on the map from Pittsburgh to Plymouth. So the distance from the real city of Pittsburgh to Plymouth must be about 500 miles.

Practice the Skill

Look at the map. Follow the directions to find distances. Use a ruler.

1 About how many inches is it on the map from Plymouth to Washington, D.C.?

2 How many miles is it from Plymouth to Washington, D.C.? Use the scale to find out.

3 A truck carries clams from Plymouth to Ithaca. How many miles does the truck travel?

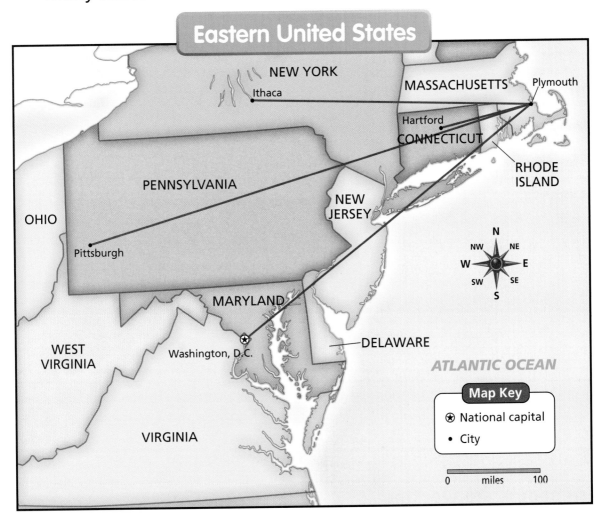

139

Goods and Services

Build on What You Know Have you ever wondered how your clothing was made or who made your toys?

Goods

The things people make or grow are called goods. **Goods** are things that you can touch, such as cars, apples, and baseballs. Many goods are made in a factory. A factory is a building where people work to make goods.

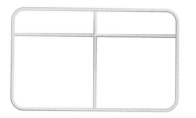

These people are working in a shoe factory.

Services

Some people are doctors, teachers, or dogwalkers. Those people do not make things. They provide services. **Services** are activities that people do to help others.

Barter

Have you ever swapped toys with a friend? That is called barter. **Barter** takes place when people trade goods or services without using money.

Long ago barter was the main way people got the things they wanted. Many times, barter does not work very well. That is why most people today pay for goods and services in other ways, often with money.

I'll give you this pig for two pounds of beets.

I'll trade one pound of beets for your pig.

Review What are some services that you use?

Scarcity and Goods and Services

People have unlimited wants for goods and services. That is why there is scarcity. **Scarcity** means we do not have enough resources to produce all the goods and services we want. We have to make choices about goods and services.

When your teacher asks your class to make a choice between two kinds of snacks, students hold up their hands to show their choice. If most students hold up their hands for raisins, the class will agree to have raisins that day. That is called majority rule. **Majority** means "the greater number" or "more than half." The chart on page 143 shows other ways to get goods and services.

The teacher tallied the children's choices for snacks.

Sharing

First come, first served

Contests

Goods and Services

Lottery

Command

Review What are some ways you get goods and services?

Lesson Review

1 Vocabulary What are some **services** that you use?

2 Main Idea What is one way that goods are different from services?

HANDS ON **Activity** Make a picture book about how people get goods and services.

SCIENTISTS SERVING OTHERS

Some scientists discover things that help many people.

Marie Curie had a good memory that helped her as a student in Poland. When she grew up, she became a scientist. She lived and worked in France with her husband Pierre. Together, they made some big discoveries. Other scientists built on their work to find ways of curing sick people and making energy.

Louis Pasteur (LOO ee pas TUR) When Louis Pasteur was a boy, his teacher saw that Louis was patient and hardworking. Later, those qualities helped Pasteur become one of France's most famous scientists. He found that heating milk killed germs. That made the milk safer to drink. Pasteur's discoveries have helped millions of people stay healthy. Milk is still heated today. The process is called pasteurization (pas chuhr ih ZAY shuhn).

George Washington Carver The plant scientist George Washington Carver wanted to help African American farmers make more money from the crops they grew. After many experiments and much hard work, Carver found hundreds of ways to use peanuts, soybeans, and sweet potatoes. Then, he thought, farmers could earn income by growing these plants too.

Eloy Rodriguez (ee LOY rohd REE gehs) Think on your feet. Use common sense. Eloy Rodriguez often heard that advice from his family. Now he is a scientist who studies how animals use plants to heal themselves. From this he has learned ways that plants can heal people. Also, Eloy Rodriguez gets students excited about science. He shares advice that helped him.

Activities

1. **Think About It** Why is it important to get students excited about science?

2. **Write About It** Write or tell how people's lives are better because of the work of the scientists you have read about.

Make a Table

▶ **Vocabulary**

table

A chart can help you see information easily. One kind of chart is called a table. A **table** puts information in order. A table has a title, headings, and lists of information.

Learn the Skill

Many people in Georgia work at service jobs. Many others work in factories making goods or products. Look at the table on page 149. It shows some factory products made in Georgia. The steps below will help you make your own table.

Step 1 The table has a title. What is the title of the table on page 149?

Step 2 Each column has a heading. What are the headings?

Step 3 Look at the information. It is sorted into the columns below the headings.

Heading

Title

Column

Georgia Products

Food	Other
Peanut butter	Rugs and carpets
Canned fruits	Chemical products
Baked goods	Electrical equipment
Chicken	Paper products

Practice the Skill

Use the steps to make your own table.

1 Choose the information you would like to show in your table. On a separate sheet of paper, write the title.

2 Decide what the column headings should be and add them.

3 Put the information into the correct columns.

Spending and Saving

Vocabulary
price
bank
savings account

Reading Skill
Predict Outcomes

STANDARDS

Core
SS2E4 Spending and saving choices

Extend
SS2E4 Spending and saving choices

Build on What You Know

Suppose you are given $2.00 for helping a neighbor. What will you do with it? Will you buy something now, or keep it for later?

Prices and Choices

The amount of money you pay to buy something is the **price.** In stores, often the prices are printed on or near things that people can buy. Looking at prices helps people decide what to buy. Ken has thirty cents to buy fruit today. The prices help him make his choice.

main idea

What do you think Ken's choice will be? Why?

30¢ each   40¢ each   25¢ each

I'm saving for my children to go to college.

We're saving for a trip to Brazil.

I'm saving up to buy in-line skates.

These people tell why they are saving money.

Saving Money

Many people are careful not to spend all their income. Some save money so they can pay for what they want. They might save money in a piggy bank. A **bank** is a safe place where people keep their money.

Review Why do people save money?

A Savings Account

Most people use a bank that has many services. One service is called a **savings account.** Instead of keeping their money at home, people put it in a savings account. They let the bank use the money. In return, the bank adds a bit more money each month. That money is called interest. Interest helps the amount of money in the account grow.

Review How are banks that are businesses and banks in people's homes alike and different?

What services are in a bank?

Gina Saves

Gina has a savings account at a bank in her town. Last year she put in money every month to save for baseball camp in July. Look at the graph of Gina's account.

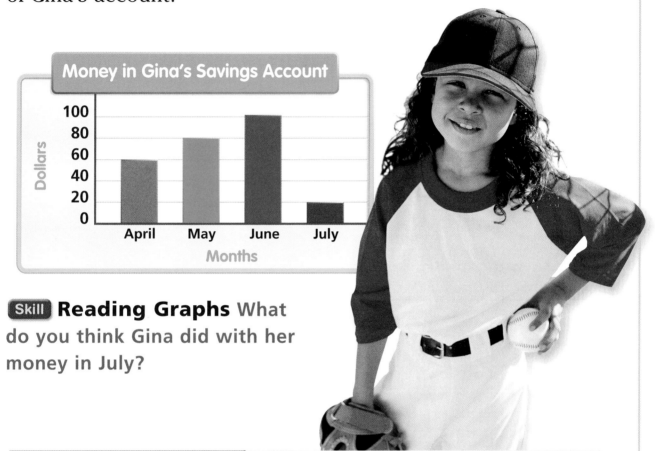

Money in Gina's Savings Account

Dollars

Months

April   May   June   July

Skill **Reading Graphs** What do you think Gina did with her money in July?

Lesson Review

❶ Vocabulary Describe a **savings account** in a bank.

❷ Main Idea What helps people make a buying choice?

Activity Write or tell about a buying choice you have made.

Spend Your Dollar

Welcome to Write On store. Take a look at what is for sale. Compare **prices.** Then see what your dollar will buy.

1 Look at the items. Choose the items you like.

2 You have only $1.00 to spend. Check the prices. See what you can buy with your $1.00.

3 Record on a class chart the items you choose. Add the prices and record the total.

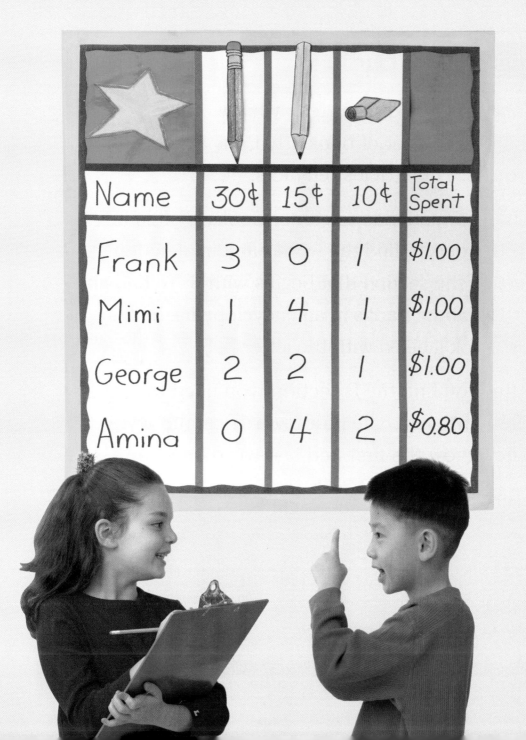

Name	30¢	15¢	10¢	Total Spent
Frank	3	0	1	$1.00
Mimi	1	4	1	$1.00
George	2	2	1	$1.00
Amina	0	4	2	$0.80

Use Reference Sources

▶ **Vocabulary**

dictionary
encyclopedia

You can find out about a topic by using reference books. There are different kinds of reference books.

Learn the Skill

A **dictionary** is a book that tells what words mean. An **encyclopedia** is a set of books that has articles on different topics. The articles tell facts.

Step 1 The information in reference books is often in ABC order. To find the word **bank** in a dictionary, look in the section that begins with B. To find an article about **banks** in an encyclopedia, look in the book labeled with the letter B.

Step 2 After you find the B section, you need to find the right page. The **guidewords** can help you. They show the first and last word on each page.

Step 3 Use ABC order to find the word **bank.**

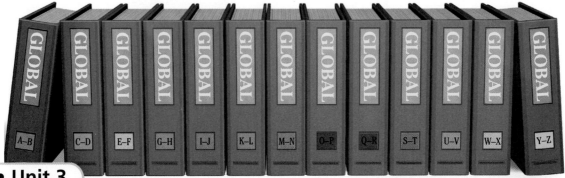

Practice the Skill

Follow the directions.

1 Suppose your teacher asks you to find information about the first factories. Tell which kind of reference book you will use.

2 Use a dictionary to find the definition of these words: **product, income, business**

Guidewords

B
b

balloon ◇ bank

balloon
A **balloon** is a kind of bag filled with gas. Some **balloons** are huge and can carry people high into the sky.

banana
A **banana** is a kind of fruit. It has a long curved shape and a yellow skin.

balloon

band

band
A **band** is a group of people who play music together. Everyone in the parade marched to the music of the **band**.

bank
A **bank** is a safe place to keep money. A **bank** can be a small box or jar that you keep at home. A **bank** is also a big building. People can leave money or borrow it at the **bank**.

20

The first word on this page is **balloon**. It is the first guideword.

The last word is **bank**. It is the second guideword.

Big Ideas

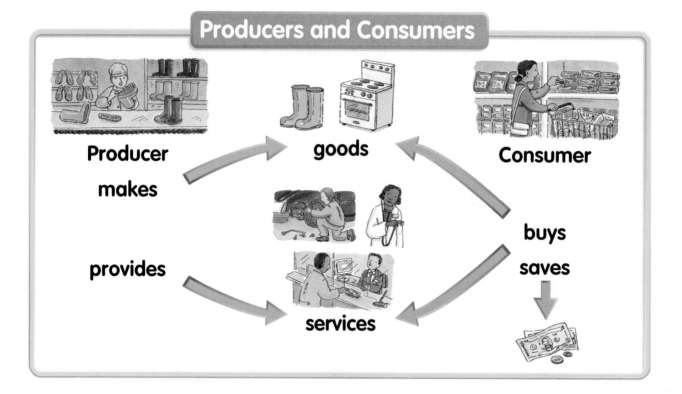

Producers and Consumers

Producer
makes
provides

goods

services

Consumer

buys
saves

Choose the missing words from the organizer.

1. A _____ makes goods.   2. A consumer buys _____ and services.   3. A consumer may _____ money in a bank.

Facts and Main Ideas

4. What is an example of opportunity cost? (page 129)

5. How do people earn income to buy what they need and want? (pages 134–135)

6. Why was Jackie Robinson's job hard? (page 136)

7. What did Jackie Robinson do to stand up for rights of African Americans? (page 136)

Vocabulary

Use words from the box to complete the sentences.

Consumers earn 8. _____
to pay for needs and 9. _____ .
One need is 10. _____ .
Consumers look at the
11. _____ of goods and
12. _____ . Consumers may
save money in a 13. _____
to pay later for things they want.

A. **prices** (page 150)

B. **income** (page 134)

C. **savings account** (page 152)

D. **services** (page 141)

E. **wants** (page 128)

F. **shelter** (page 128)

 Test Practice

14. What does the word **barter** mean?

A. earning a small income

B. saving money in a bank

C. trading without money

D. producing many goods

Critical Thinking

Main Idea and Details

15. Why do most people use money to get things they want?

16. Tell the opportunity cost and the benefit of a spending and a saving choice you made.

Review and Test Prep

Skillbuilders Use a Map Scale

17. On this map, one inch equals _____ .

18. How far is it from Maria's house to the airport?

Use Reference Sources

19. Which reference book would you use to find the meaning of the word **income?**

20. If you want to look up information about business, which encyclopedia book will you choose?

Connect to Georgia

Unit Activity

GEORGIA

Make a Mobile

If you earned $10, how much of your money would you spend and save?

❶ Write and draw your choices.

❷ Make sure that they add up to $10.

❸ Cut out your choices and hang them up to make a mobile. Explain your choices.

Personal Finance

GEORGIA

You have $15 and want to buy a $12 game and a $13 book. Which one would you choose? Why? What is the opportunity cost of your choice?

CURRENT EVENTS

WEEKLY (WR) READER

Current Events Project

Find articles about jobs around the world. Publish a **Class Newspaper** about people at work around the world.

Technology

Read articles about current events at **www.eduplace.com/kids/hmss/**

American Heroes
Read About It

Learn more about Jackie Robinson in his biography.

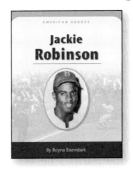

America's Government

66 **We are as free as we dare to be.** 99

—Andrew Young, Georgia leader

The **Big** Idea

What does government mean to you and your family?

Unit 4 — America's Government

Vocabulary Preview

Technology
e • **glossary**
e • **word games**
www.eduplace.com/kids/hmss/

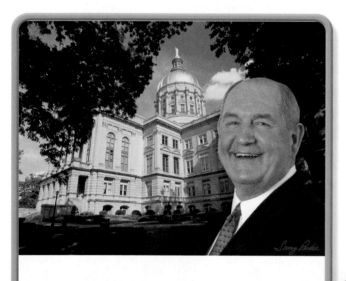

government

A **government** needs a leader and a group of people who work together to run a community, state, or nation. page 168

citizen

A **citizen** is a member of a community, state, or country. You are a citizen of your class too. page 188

Reading Strategy

Use the **summarize** reading strategy in Lessons 1, 2, and 3 and the **question** strategy in Lessons 4 and 5.

election

An **election** is a time when people vote. You can hold a class election to make a choice. page 196

Constitution

The **Constitution** is a plan for making rules for the United States government. page 202

A New Country

Vocabulary

independence
government

Reading Skill

Sequence

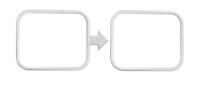

Build on What You Know Have you had to follow rules that didn't seem fair to you?

Many Colonies

Europeans built colonies up and down the eastern coast of North America. In those colonies, they built homes and churches. They started farms and businesses. Some small communities grew into large towns and cities. People in communities worked and planned together. But the colonists still had to follow rules from the king of England in Great Britain.

main idea

The map shows thirteen of the British colonies in North America in 1763. Georgia was the farthest south.

Review Where was Georgia colony located?

STANDARDS

SS2CG1 Concept of government
    Historical Understanding
GPS Information Processing Skill 5: Sequence,
    cause and effect
GPS Information Processing Skill 7: Timelines

The Thirteen Colonies

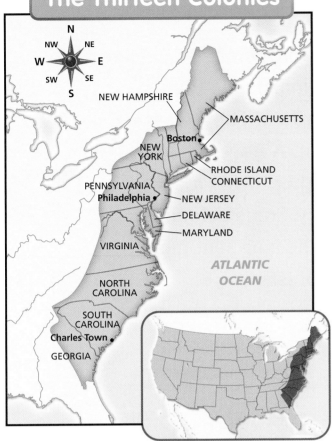

NEW HAMPSHIRE
MASSACHUSETTS
Boston
NEW YORK
RHODE ISLAND
CONNECTICUT
PENNSYLVANIA
Philadelphia
NEW JERSEY
DELAWARE
MARYLAND
VIRGINIA
ATLANTIC OCEAN
NORTH CAROLINA
SOUTH CAROLINA
Charles Town
GEORGIA

N NE NW W E SW SE S

Boston

Charles Town

Philadelphia

Independence

Independence means being free from rule by another country. More and more colonists in America wanted independence from Great Britain. They wanted to run their own government. A **government** is a group of people who work together to run a community, county, state, or country. Some colonists began to act against British rules. The king sent more and more armies to control the colonists.

April 1775
British army fights with colonists in Massachusetts

1770   1775

The Declaration of Independence

People from the thirteen colonies did not all agree about independence from Great Britain. Each colony sent people to Philadelphia to meet and make a decision. People at the meeting chose Thomas Jefferson to write an explanation of why the colonies wanted independence. His explanation is called the Declaration of Independence. By signing the Declaration, colonists showed that they agreed with one another on the goal of independence.

main idea ★

Review What did colonists do that showed they wanted independence?

July 1776
Thirteen colonies agree on the Declaration of Independence

1776   1780

This painting shows an artist's idea of how George Washington looked when he crossed the Delaware River during the American Revolution.

The American Revolution

Great Britain would not allow independence. The king sent soldiers to fight a war against the colonists. The war was called the American Revolution. George Washington led the soldiers who fought against Britain. There were terrible battles. The American Revolution lasted eight years. Finally in 1783, the war ended. The colonies had won independence. They formed a country called the United States of America, with its own government.

main
★
idea

Leaders for Independence

You have read how George Washington and Thomas Jefferson helped America gain independence. Many others helped too. **Benjamin Franklin** got colonists to think and talk about why they wanted independence. **Abigail Adams** wrote what she saw and thought about the fight for independence. **Samuel Adams** made speeches that got many colonists to fight for independence.

Benjamin Franklin

Review Why did colonists fight in the American Revolution?

Samuel Adams

Lesson Review

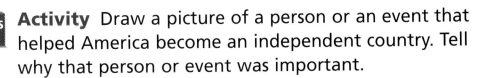

❶ **Vocabulary** Write a sentence to tell how colonists won **independence** and formed a country **government.**

❷ **Main Idea** Why was the Declaration of Independence important to the colonists?

HANDS ON **Activity** Draw a picture of a person or an event that helped America become an independent country. Tell why that person or event was important.

Primary Source

Abigail Adams

Abigail Adams always loved to write long letters. She described events in exciting detail and shared her own ideas.

Abigail married John Adams, who was a leader in the American Revolution. He often traveled far from home. While he was gone, Abigail ran their farm and took care of the household with very little help and not much money. Abigail wrote to John daily. She described life with their children and troubles from the war. Abigail also explained her own ideas about **independence.**

1776
Wrote about importance of women

1744
Born in Weymouth, Massachusetts

1700

1800

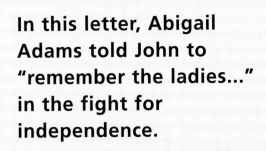

In this letter, Abigail Adams told John to "remember the ladies..." in the fight for independence.

Activities

1. **Talk About It** Choose a picture from these two pages and explain what you can learn from it.

2. **Make It** Make a poster that shows something important about the life of Abigail Adams.

Reading and Thinking Skills

Tell Fact from Opinion

▶ **Vocabulary**

fact

opinion

A **fact** is something that is true. An **opinion** is what someone thinks. Two people can have different opinions about the same facts.

> Independence Day is on July 4 every year.

> I think Independence Day is our country's best holiday.

Learn the Skill

Step 1 Read the sentences about Independence Day. One sentence tells a fact. The other sentence tells an opinion.

Step 2 A fact is something that is true. You can check to see if a fact is true. A fact is probably true if two or more good nonfiction books agree.

Step 3 Opinions use words such as "I think."

STANDARDS

GPS Information Processing Skill 4:
Fact and opinion

Practice the Skill

Read the sentences below each picture. Then follow the directions.

1 In what way is a fact different from an opinion?

2 Which sentences below tell facts?

3 Which sentence below tells an opinion? Tell how you know that it is an opinion.

George Washington was the first President of our country.

John Hancock's signature is the largest on the Declaration of Independence.

I think Benjamin Franklin was the greatest inventor of all time.

Government and People

Build on What You Know

Who are the people who work together to help run your school?

Government

Countries, states, and communities are like schools. Each is run by a group of people working together. Each of those groups is a government.

Vocabulary

capitol

capital

tax

Reading Skill

Draw Conclusions

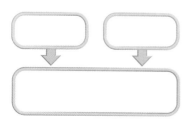

STANDARDS

Core
SS2CG1 Concept of government
SS2CG4a State capitol building; state and national
    capitals

Extend
GPS Information Processing Skill 3:
    Problems and solutions

People in a community government work in the town or city hall.

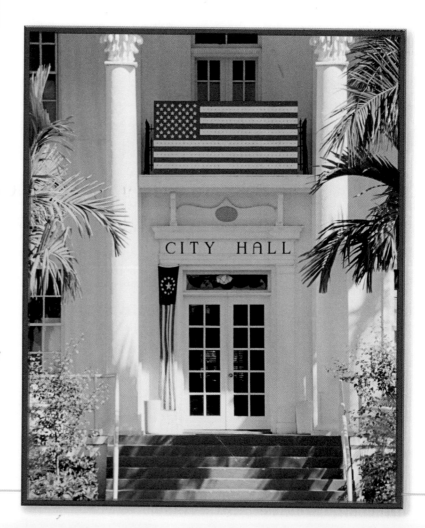

The government of Georgia meets in this building in Atlanta.

Georgia's Local and State Governments

The government of a community is called a local government. People in your local government work in the town or city hall and in other places in the community.

People in Georgia's state government meet in the building above. It is called a **capitol.**

Review Where do people in government meet?

Kinds of Government

Each state has a **capital,** which is the city where the people in state government work. Atlanta is your state capital. The United States government is called the national government. It is in Washington, D.C., the nation's capital. Everyone has three kinds of governments: local, state, and national.

Look at Robin, for example.

I live in Augusta, Georgia. Leaders of my **local** government meet in Augusta.

Leaders of my **state** government meet in Atlanta, the capital of Georgia.

Leaders of my **national** government meet in Washington, D.C.

The United States of America

North
NW | NE
West | East
SW | SE
South

CANADA

NORTH DAKOTA
★Bismarck

MINNESOTA
St. Paul ★

SOUTH DAKOTA
Pierre ★

WISCONSIN
Madison ★

MICHIGAN
★ Lansing

Cheyenne ★

NEBRASKA

Lincoln ★

IOWA
Des Moines ★

ILLINOIS
Springfield ★

INDIANA
Indianapolis ★

OHIO
Columbus ★

Denver ★

COLORADO

Topeka ★

KANSAS

MISSOURI
Jefferson City ★

KENTUCKY
Frankfort ★

WEST VIRGINIA
Charleston ★

VIRGINIA
Richmond ★

NEW HAMPSHIRE
VERMONT
Montpelier ★

MAINE
Augusta ★

MASSACHUSETTS
Concord ★
★ Boston

Albany ★

NEW YORK

★ Providence
RHODE ISLAND

Hartford ★
CONNECTICUT

PENNSYLVANIA
Harrisburg ★

★ Trenton
NEW JERSEY

Annapolis ⊛

Dover ★

DELAWARE
MARYLAND

Washington, D.C.

Raleigh ★

NORTH CAROLINA

ATLANTIC OCEAN

OKLAHOMA
Oklahoma City ★

ARKANSAS
Little Rock ★

TENNESSEE
Nashville ★

Columbia ★
SOUTH CAROLINA

Atlanta ★
Augusta •
GEORGIA

MISSISSIPPI
Jackson ★

ALABAMA
Montgomery ★

LOUISIANA

TEXAS

Austin ★

Baton Rouge ★

★ Tallahassee

FLORIDA

MEXICO

Gulf of Mexico

Map Key
- • Robin's city
- ★ State capital
- ⊛ National capital
- — State boundary
- — National boundary

Skill **Reading Maps** Find Augusta, Georgia. Is Augusta east, or west, of the state capital of Georgia?

Government Services

Remember the services you read about in Unit 3. Fixing cars and cutting hair are services. Governments have many services for people too. Local, state, and national governments each help with different services. Here are some examples.

(★) main idea

Services

Local Government

schools
firefighters
libraries
police

State Government

state colleges
state parks
state roads

National Government

National Park Service
U.S. Post Office
Coast Guard

Taxes

How do governments pay for services? Governments collect money called **taxes.** Workers pay income taxes from the money they earn. Businesses also pay income taxes. In Georgia and most other states, people pay sales taxes when they buy goods such as bikes or baseballs.

main idea

Review Why do governments need taxes?

Baseball Bat	35.00
Baseball	8.00
Baseball glove	40.00
SUBTOTAL	83.00
Georgia Tax 4.00%	3.32
TOTAL	$86.32
Cash	90.00
Cash Change	3.68

Lesson Review

1 Vocabulary Write a sentence that explains what **taxes** are.

2 Main Idea What are the three governments that people have?

Activity Write or tell about a local government service you use. Explain how it helps you and other people.

Solving Problems

People in communities have problems to solve. Sometimes people in schools do, too. Read about some students who try to solve a problem at their school.

Cast

Narrator

Lisa: student

Greg: student

Mimi: student

Don: student

Mr. Vacca: teacher

Ms. Leroy: principal

Scene 1

Narrator: We are in Mr. Vacca's classroom. It's a Friday in April. Our class is almost ready to go home. Then the principal, Ms. Leroy, speaks on the intercom.

Ms. Leroy: Next week the builders will start the new addition to our school. They will have to take out all the bike racks. After that, no one can ride a bike to school.

Lisa: So we can't ride our bikes to school all spring!

Mr. Vacca: Everyone listen, please!

Ms. Leroy: Please make sure to take my letter home to your families. It tells why students cannot ride bikes to school.

Mr. Vacca: Now everyone may go, quietly! Have a good weekend.

Don: How can we have a good weekend with bad news like that?

Mimi: Maybe it will be good if we can solve the bike problem!

Lisa: Let's meet at the bike racks to talk about it.

Scene 2

Narrator: Lisa, Greg, Mimi, and Don meet at the bike racks.

Lisa: First we have to name the problem.

Greg: The problem is we want to ride our bikes to school, but now we can't.

Lisa: Next we should name the reasons why we can't ride our bikes.

Greg: Because they're building where the bike racks are.

Mimi: Then let's tell them not to build!

Don: But we want them to build. They are building a theater and a new gym.

Mimi: What if we hid Ms. Leroy's letter from our families and rode our bikes anyway?

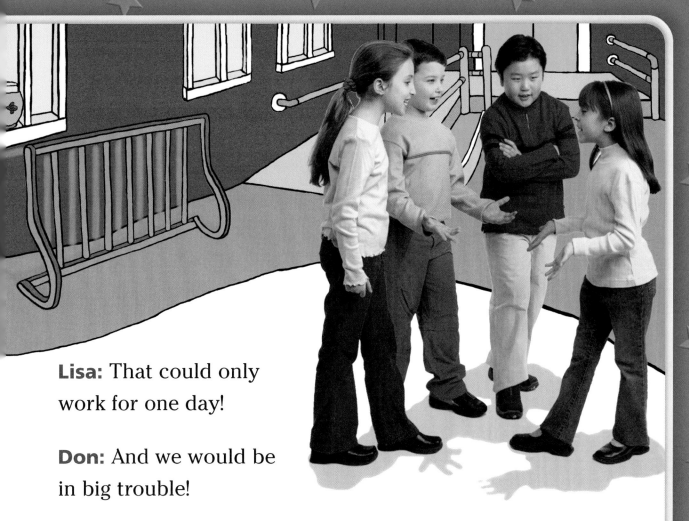

Lisa: That could only work for one day!

Don: And we would be in big trouble!

Greg: Here's another idea. Maybe they can move the bike racks to the other side of the school.

Lisa: That should work! Let's go talk to Ms. Leroy.

Don: I'll bet she'll listen. Maybe she can help us think of another way to solve the problem if our idea doesn't work.

Activities

1. **Think About It** Do you like the way the students tried to solve the problem? Why?

2. **Write About It** Write or tell what Ms. Leroy might say when the students talk to her.

Skillbuilder

Solve a Problem

People in classrooms and communities don't always agree. When people disagree, it is called a **conflict.** Together, people can solve conflicts and other problems.

▶ **Vocabulary**

conflict

Learn the Skill

Follow the steps to help solve a problem.

Step 1 Look at the picture. Describe the conflict. Two children want to use the computer at the same time.

Step 2 Think about what each child wants to do.

Write	Play Games

Step 3 Think of ways to solve the problem.

- Take turns.
- Writer uses pencil.
- Game player plays board game.

Step 4 Ask yourself about each idea: Can both children do some of what they want? Choose the best way to solve the problem.

Practice the Skill

STANDARDS

GPS Information Processing Skill 3:
Problems and solutions

Work with a small group. Look at the picture below. Then follow the directions.

1 Tell in your own words what the conflict is. What does each group want?

2 List some ways to solve the problem.

3 Choose the best solution. Tell why your solution is the best one.

Citizens Make a Difference

Vocabulary

citizen
right
responsibility
law

Reading Skill

Classify

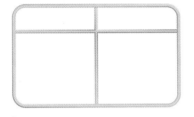

STANDARDS

Core
SS2CG1 Concept of government/need for laws

Extend
SS2H1a Contribution of Martin Luther King, Jr.
SS2CG3 Character trait: liberty

Build on What You Know

Think of ways students have made your school a good place to learn. You will read about how you are a citizen in your school, community, and nation.

You Are a Citizen

A **citizen** is a person who belongs to a place. You are a citizen of the community where you live and the nation where you were born. You can also become a citizen of the United States even if you were not born here.

Citizens Have Rights

As a citizen, you have rights that the government protects. A **right** is something you may do. As a citizen of the United States, you have a right to speak freely and to practice your religion. In the past, American Indians, African Americans, and women were not treated fairly. They had to speak out for their right to to be treated fairly. Martin Luther King, Jr., was a leader in the fight for equal rights.

Review What rights do you have as a citizen?

189

Citizens Have Responsibilities

Along with rights, citizens have responsibilities.  A **responsibility** is something that you should do. A responsibility may be following rules or doing a chore. It may be treating others fairly. Name some responsibilities you have. What would happen if you did not do them?

Skill **Reading Visuals** What are the citizens doing for their community?

Responsibilities, Rules, and Laws

A responsibility everyone has is to obey (oh BAY) rules and laws. You follow rules at home and in school. A **law** is a rule that everyone in a community, state, or country must follow. Laws in Georgia and other states keep people safe and help them get along with one another. What do you think would happen if Georgia had no traffic laws?

main idea ★

Review Why are rules and laws important?

The signs on this page tell people about laws.

Police in Georgia and other states stop
drivers who speed.

Police Help with Laws

Local, state, and national governments have laws.
Police help with government laws. They tell people
how to obey laws. They stop people who break laws.
Look at the picture on this page. What do you think is
happening? Think of another way that police help
with laws.

main idea (★)

Citizens Help with Laws

Citizens protect each other when they know and follow laws. When people obey a traffic law, they help keep others safe. When you follow laws in a park, you help others enjoy the park. Citizens help by choosing good people to make laws. Citizens can also work together to make better laws.

States have laws about driving. In Georgia, you must be fifteen before you can get a permit to learn to drive.

Review What can citizens do to help with laws?

Lesson Review

1 Vocabulary Name two **rights** of **citizens** in the United States.

2 Main Idea Copy this sentence. Fill in the blanks. Citizens of the United States have _____ and _____.

Activity Name a law that you think is important. Write or tell why you think it is important.

Martin Luther King, Jr.

Martin Luther King, Jr., helped to change the way Americans lived together. When he was a boy, African Americans could not go to the same schools or eat in the same places as other people did. King worked to change that.

King gave speeches about liberty, or freedom. He once said,

"Let freedom ring."

King wanted all Americans to share the same rights and freedoms stated in the United States Constitution.

In 1963, more than 200,000 people listened to King speak at a march in Washington, D.C.

Biographies!
Read more about
Martin Luther King, Jr.

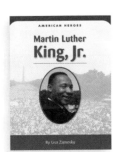

Activities

1. **THINK ABOUT IT** Why do you think so many people wanted to hear Martin Luther King, Jr., speak?

2. **DRAW IT** We celebrate Martin Luther King, Jr.'s, birthday with a holiday on the third Monday in January. Draw a way that you could celebrate the day.

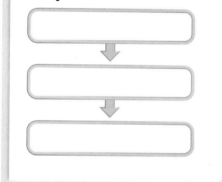

Core Lesson 4

Vocabulary

vote
election
mayor
governor
president

Reading Skill

Sequence

```

```
↓
```

```
↓
```

```

```

STANDARDS

Core
SS2CG2a Role of President
SS2CG2b Role of governor
SS2CG2c Role of mayor

Extend
SS2H1a Contribution of Jimmy Carter: leadership, human rights
SS2CG3 Character trait: compassion

Our Leaders

Build on What You Know

Sports teams and school bands have leaders. What are some other kinds of leaders? Governments have leaders too.

Choosing Leaders

Did you ever choose a leader for a team? When you show or write a choice, you **vote.** Your school might have an **election,** which is a time when people vote. When you turn eighteen, you will have the right to vote in government elections. You may vote for many different leaders in one election. The chart shows three examples.
```

Government Leaders

Mayor

The role of a **mayor** is to lead a city or town government.

Governor

The role of a **governor** is to lead a state government.

President

The role of a **President** is to lead our country, the United States of America.

People in government have important jobs. Some are leaders. Others make laws. Still others make sure the laws work well. In elections, citizens get to choose people who they think can do these jobs the best.

main idea

Review Why should citizens vote in government elections?

Before You Vote

What can citizens do to choose the best leaders? They can read newspapers and watch television. They can ask questions of leaders. They can ask themselves questions.

Will you add more bus stops?

What can you do to fix our playgrounds?

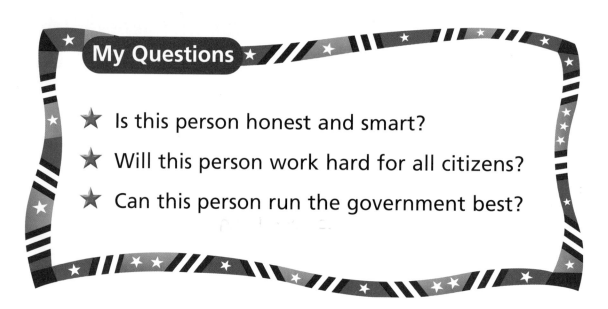

My Questions

★ Is this person honest and smart?

★ Will this person work hard for all citizens?

★ Can this person run the government best?

Leaders and Citizens

Leaders who win elections need to keep listening to citizens. Citizens need to keep telling leaders what they want for their community, state, and country. Citizens and their leaders together help governments work well.

Review Why should leaders talk with citizens?

Lesson Review

❶ Vocabulary Use the words **vote** and **election** to tell some things you know about leaders.

❷ Main Idea Tell something that government leaders do.

Activity Write or tell two things a voter can do before an election.

Jimmy Carter

Jimmy Carter began as a farmer and became President. Carter was the governor of Georgia for four years too. In 1976, he became the thirty-ninth President of the United States.

Jimmy Carter didn't stop there. He and his wife Rosalynn Carter started the Carter Center. The center works for peace, fights disease, and brings hope to people around the world. The work of the center shows Carter's compassion, or caring, for others. Once he said,

"We can choose to [stop] suffering. We can choose to work together for peace. We can make these changes—and we must."

★ A Georgia Hero ★

President Carter helped the leaders of Egypt and Israel agree to peace.

Biographies!
Read more about Jimmy Carter.

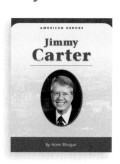

Activities

1. **THINK ABOUT IT** What is one way Jimmy Carter shows compassion for others?

2. **WRITE ABOUT IT** Write a paragraph. Describe a good leader you know.

Core Lesson 5

National Government

Vocabulary

Constitution
democracy
liberty
justice

Reading Skill

Classify

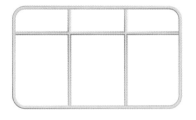

STANDARDS

SS2CG1 Concept of government
SS2CG4a National capitol building
SS2CG4b National capital

Build on What You Know

When you start a class project, you may write a plan for how it will work. In a way, that is like the plan that early leaders wrote for our nation's government.

A Plan for Government

In Lesson 1 you read about the American Revolution. When that war ended, American leaders did not want a king to rule the new nation. The leaders met and wrote a new plan for the government. That plan is called the **Constitution.**

(main ★ idea)

Review What is the Constitution?

202 • Unit 4

Skill **Visual Learning** Leaders worked on the Constitution in Philadelphia in 1787. What do you think the people are talking about?

Important Words

The writers of the Constitution planned a **democracy,** which is government by the people. They used words that they believed were important in a democracy. One word was **liberty,** which means "freedom." Another was **justice,** which means "fairness." Why are they still important words today?

Government in Three Parts

The Constitution is more than 200 years old. It is still the plan for our government today. The Constitution describes a government in three parts, or branches. Each branch has its own building in Washington, D.C. On these pages you can read about the people who work in those buildings.

main idea ★

Review How many branches does the government have?

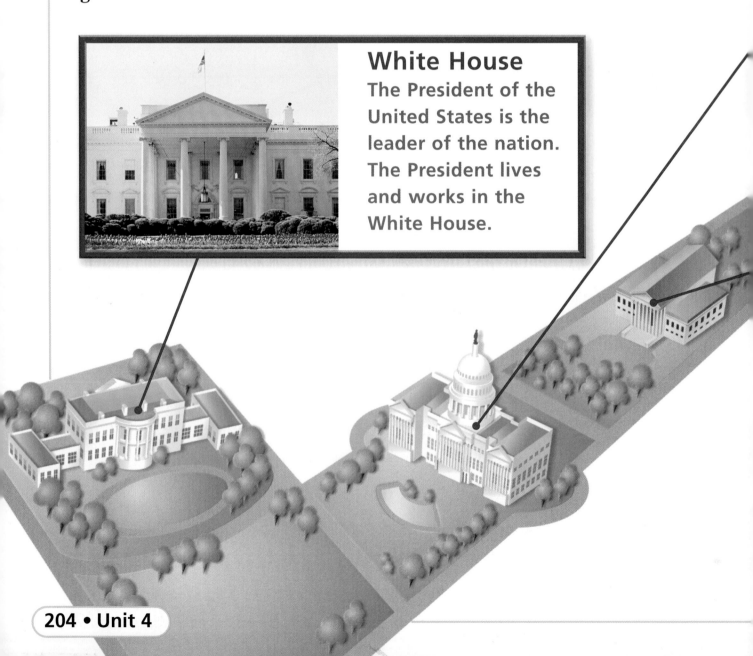

White House
The President of the United States is the leader of the nation. The President lives and works in the White House.

Capitol

The members of Congress make laws. Men and women in Congress come from all fifty states. They work in the Capitol Building.

Supreme Court

The Supreme Court has nine judges who look carefully at laws. They decide if the laws are fair and protect citizens' rights. They meet in the Supreme Court Building.

Lesson Review

❶ **Vocabulary** When do you say, "with **liberty** and **justice** for all"? Tell what it means.

❷ **Main Idea** What are three buildings that are part of the national government?

Activity Make a chart that shows who works in the three branches of government.

Democracy

Democracy is government that comes from the people. In a democracy, people make choices about their leaders and their laws. They may do this by voting in an election.

In the United States, citizens age 18 or older may vote for a leader of their community or state. They may also vote for a few people from their state to go to Washington, D.C. Those people are members of Congress. Georgia sends 13 people to the United States Congress. In Congress, these people vote to make laws for all the citizens in the country. Look at examples of democracy in the United States.

School

Students vote on where to have their class picnic.

Community

This city council in Kingsland, Georgia, votes on how much money to spend on city services.

Democracy in Action

Nation

People vote for a President of the United States.

State

People hear speeches before they vote for governor of Georgia.

Activities

1. **Talk About It** Tell how democracy is part of what happens in your class or school.

2. **Write About It** Write about why voting is important in a democracy.

207

Map and Globe Skills

Compare Maps

▶ **Vocabulary**

county seat

Georgia has natural places such as rivers, lakes, and mountains. It has cities, counties, museums, and parks, too. All these things and more can be shown on maps. There are different maps for different purposes.

Learn the Skill

Both maps on the next page show Sumter County. Map A shows some natural places in the county. This kind of map is called a physical map. Map B shows places such as towns and county borders. It shows the **county seat,** which is the town where county government meets and works. This map shows a museum, too. This kind of map is called a political map.

Step 1 Look at Map A. What natural places does it show?

Step 2 Look at Map B. Which cities and towns do you see?

Step 3 Find the museum on Map B. Why is this place not shown on Map A?

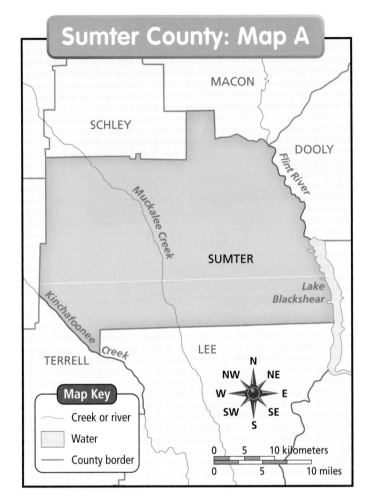

Sumter County: Map A

MACON

SCHLEY

DOOLY

Flint River

Muckalee Creek

SUMTER

Lake Blackshear

Kinchafoonee Creek

TERRELL

LEE

N
NW   NE
W   E
SW   SE
S

Map Key
~ Creek or river
▢ Water
— County border

0   5   10 kilometers
0   5   10 miles

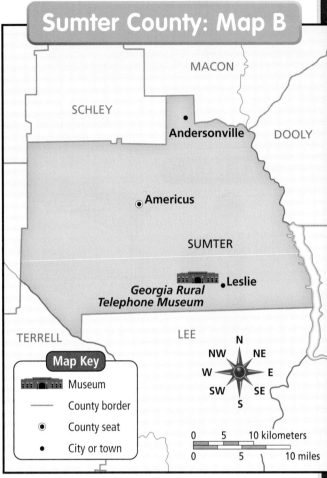

Sumter County: Map B

MACON

SCHLEY

• Andersonville

DOOLY

⊙ Americus

SUMTER

 • Leslie
Georgia Rural Telephone Museum

TERRELL

LEE

N
NW   NE
W   E
SW   SE
S

Map Key
🏛 Museum
— County border
⊙ County seat
• City or town

0   5   10 kilometers
0   5   10 miles

Which map gives information about natural places? The map below shows where Sumter County is in Georgia.

STANDARDS

GPS Map and Globe Skill 4: Compare and contrast maps

GEORGIA

SUMTER COUNTY

Practice the Skill

Look at the two maps. Then answer the questions.

1 On which map would you add Andersonville National Historic Site? Why?

2 On which map would you add a river? Why?

Big Ideas

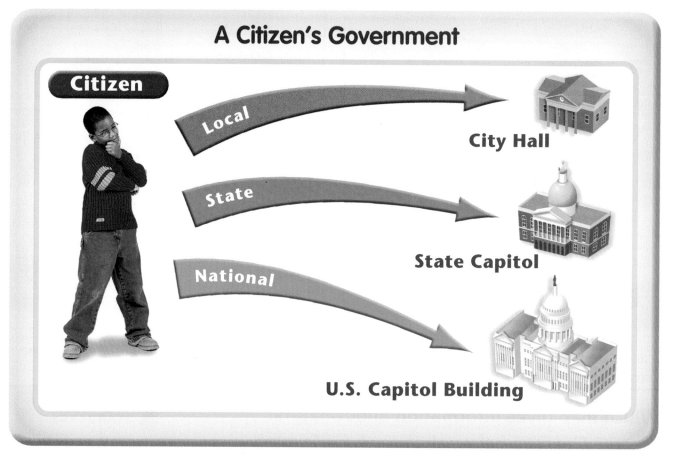

A Citizen's Government

Citizen

Local → City Hall

State → State Capitol

National → U.S. Capitol Building

Fill in three missing words that help describe the chart.

Each citizen has 1. _____ , 2. _____ , and 3. _____ governments.
(page 178)

Facts and Main Ideas

4. Where is the national government? (page 178)

5. What is one responsibility that citizens have? (page 190)

6. Why are laws important? (page 191)

7. What are two things citizens can do to choose good leaders? (page 198)

Vocabulary

Write the letter of the correct answer.

8. The money that people pay to a government

9. A person who belongs to a place

10. A freedom that government must protect

11. A time when people vote

A. **right** (page 189)

B. **election** (page 196)

C. **taxes** (page 181)

D. **citizen** (page 188)

E. **capital** (page 178)

 Test Practice

12. What does the word **government** mean?

    A. A person who belongs to a place, such as a state

    B. A group of people who make and carry out laws

    C. A leader of a community, state, or country

    D. Something that people should do for others

Critical Thinking

Compare and Contrast

13. What are some ways that your local government is like the national government and different from it?

14. What is one way Martin Luther King, Jr., and Jimmy Carter have each helped people?

Review and Test Prep

Compare Fact and Opinion

A fact is something that is true. An opinion is what someone thinks. Look at the poster and answer the questions.

15. Which sentence below tells a fact?
16. Which sentence below is an opinion?

   A. I think Tina would be a good class president.

   B. Tina is running for class president.

Solve a Problem

Jack, Darryl, Lena, and Kay all want another slice of pizza. There are only 2 slices of pizza left.

17. Choose the best way to solve the problem.

A   B   C

Connect to Georgia

Unit Activity GEORGIA

Make Up a Riddle

Think of a person, place, or thing you learned about in this unit. You might choose a government leader or service worker. Keep your choice secret.

❶ Fold a sheet of paper in half and write two riddle clues on the outside. Write your secret answer inside.

❷ Show your clues to others. Can they guess?

MY Clues
1. a plan
2. rights

CURRENT EVENTS
WEEKLY (WR) READER

Weekly Reader Project

Find out what your local government is doing. Make a **Government in the News** big book.

Government in the News

Technology

Read articles about current events at **www.eduplace.com/kids/hmss/**

Personal Finance GEORGIA

Suppose you are saving money to buy something. How does Georgia's sales tax affect the amount you need to save?

American Heroes
Read About It

Learn more about these leaders in their biographies.

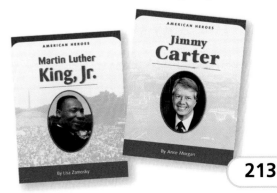

AMERICAN HEROES
Martin Luther King, Jr.
By Lisa Zamosky

AMERICAN HEROES
Jimmy Carter
By Anne Morgan

Veterans Day

Veterans Day honors people who were in the army and other armed forces. Soldiers, sailors, and pilots who served the United States are veterans.

Many veterans march in Veterans Day parades. People thank our veterans for helping our country when it is at war and at peace.

A Purple Heart medal

Activity

Thank You Letter

1. Write a thank you letter to a veteran.

2. You may display your letter or mail it to a group of veterans.

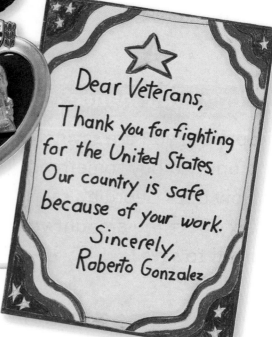

Dear Veterans,
Thank you for fighting for the United States. Our country is safe because of your work.
Sincerely,
Roberto Gonzalez

Thanksgiving

On Thanksgiving Day people give thanks for what they have. This is a tradition that comes from harvest festivals long ago. The Pilgrims shared their first harvest with the Wampanoag.

In 1863, President Abraham Lincoln thought the United States should have a day of thanks. He started the national holiday we celebrate today.

American families of many backgrounds celebrate Thanksgiving Day. People may eat foods from their own culture and also turkey and cranberry sauce. Many families talk about why they feel thankful. Some go to church.

Activity

Thanksgiving Stick Puppets

1. Make stick puppets of the Pilgrims and the Wampanoag.

2. What do you think the Pilgrims and the Wampanoag felt thankful for? Use the puppets to act out your ideas.

215

January

Martin Luther King, Jr. Day

Dr. Martin Luther King, Jr., worked to make laws that would be fair to all people. Each year, Americans honor his work.

Like many people, Dr. King knew that some laws were not fair to African Americans. He gave speeches and marched to show the need to change the unfair laws. He shared his dream of good lives for all. He received the Nobel Peace Prize for his work.

friendship

Activity

Dream Doves

peace

1. Think of a dream that you believe is good for everyone.

2. Write your dream on the shape of a dove.

happiness

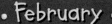

Presidents' Day

On Presidents' Day, people honor two important Presidents of the United States.

George Washington helped make the United States a free country. He led the army for the new country in the American Revolution. He was the first President of the United States.

Abraham Lincoln was another great President. He helped to make all people in the United States equal and free. Lincoln helped keep the states together in one country.

Activity

"If I Am President" Poster

1. Think about what you would do if you were the President of the United States.

2. Make a poster to show your ideas.

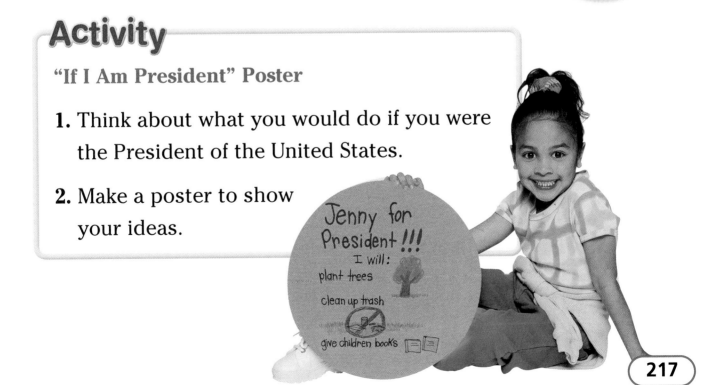

Jenny for President!!!
I will:
plant trees
clean up trash
give children books

Memorial Day

Vietnam Veterans Memorial

On Memorial Day, citizens of the United States remember the people who fought and died in wars.

A memorial is something that helps people remember a person, a group, or an event from the past. A memorial can be a statue, a sign, or a building. On Memorial Day, people gather at memorials and cemeteries.

People put flowers and flags on memorials and graves. Towns and cities have parades or speeches. Citizens honor the people who fought for the United States.

Activity

Make a Memorial Circle

1. Think of a person or an event you want to remember.

2. Write the words on a circle of colored paper. You may add a picture.

In memory of my grandpa Ted Barrios

In memory of people who fought in all wars

Flag Day

The United States flag stands for our country. On Flag Day, many communities have parades and sing the national anthem.

Our country's first flag had only 13 stripes and 13 stars. They stood for the 13 colonies that formed our country. Later the colonies became states.

Now there are 50 states in the United States. The United States flag has 50 stars that stand for our 50 states. It still has 13 stripes.

Activity

State Stars

1. Cut out the shape of a white star.

2. Write the name of a state in red. Write the capital of the state in blue.

Tallahassee Florida

Springfield Illinois

Atlanta Georgia

Independence Day

On the Fourth of July, we celebrate our country's birthday.

The United States was born on July 4, 1776. On that day, our leaders signed an important paper. It said that our land and our people were now free from Great Britain.

Independence is another word for **freedom.** Every Fourth of July, we celebrate our country's freedom. Towns and cities have parades and picnics. Many communities have fireworks at night.

Activity

Freedom Poem

1. Think of some things that United States citizens are free to do.

2. Write a poem about your freedoms. You may start with the words "I am free. . . ."

I am free to read books and talk to people.

I am free to think and learn.

I am free to be me!

References

Citizenship Handbook

Resources

Our Flag

Pledge of Allegiance

I **pledge allegiance** to the flag
of the United States of America
and to the **Republic** for which it stands,
one Nation under God, **indivisible,**
with **liberty** and **justice** for all.

**What does the Pledge of Allegiance mean?
Use the vocabulary to explain.**

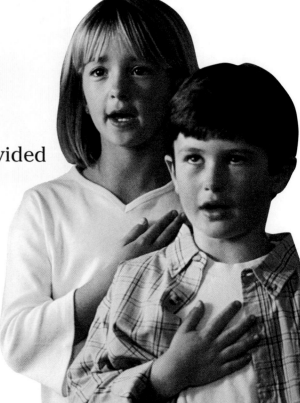

pledge: promise
republic: nation
liberty: freedom
allegiance: loyalty
indivisible: cannot be divided
justice: fairness

Rules about the Flag

Look at some rules about our national flag. They come from a law called the United States Flag Code.

- The flag should have thirteen stripes, red and white. It should have white stars on a blue background. It should have a star for each state.

- To salute the flag, stand straight and face the flag. Put your right hand on your heart.

- Say the pledge while you salute.

- Do not let the flag touch the ground.

- Fly the United States flag above any state flag.

- At night, take down the flag or light it up.

Songs of Our Nation

Many songs show our pride in our country. How did they come to be?

In 1893, a teacher from the East named Katharine Lee Bates took a trip to the West. The beauty of mountains, plains, and open skies inspired her to write a poem. Bates's poem became the words for the song "America the Beautiful."

"America the Beautiful"

by Katharine Lee Bates

O beautiful for spacious skies,
For amber waves of grain,
For purple mountain majesties
Above the fruited plain.
America! America!
God shed His grace on thee
And crown thy good with brotherhood
From sea to shining sea.

Vocabulary

spacious: spread over a large area

amber: golden brown

majesties: powers

fruited: successfully planted

shed: give out

grace: blessing

thee: you

brotherhood: friendship

What does the song mean to you? The words above help explain the song.

Samuel F. Smith heard the British national anthem in 1832 and liked the music. He wrote words so that Americans could sing it. "America," or "My Country, 'Tis of Thee," quickly became a favorite of many people in the United States. People still love to sing it today.

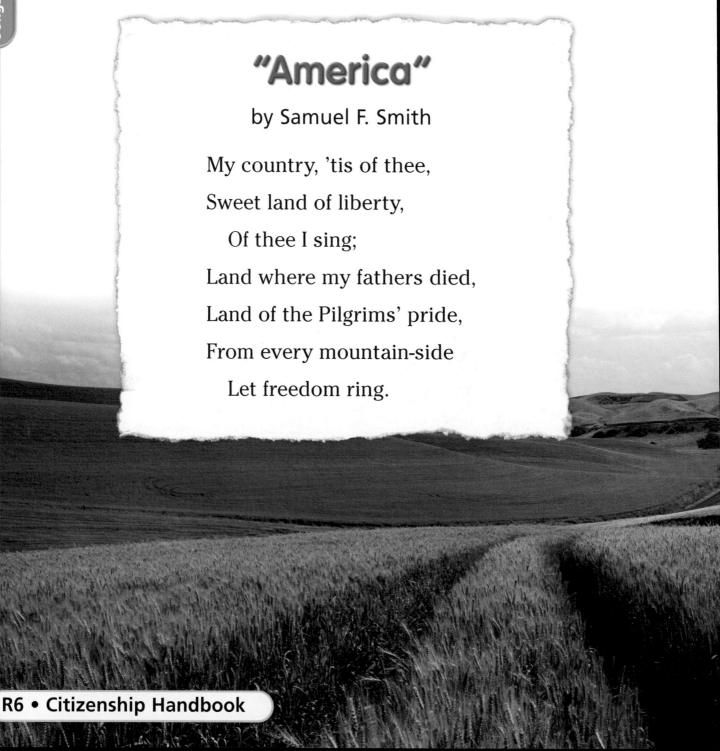

"America"

by Samuel F. Smith

My country, 'tis of thee,

Sweet land of liberty,

Of thee I sing;

Land where my fathers died,

Land of the Pilgrims' pride,

From every mountain-side

Let freedom ring.

Irving Berlin first wrote "God Bless America" for a show in 1918 but did not use it then. Twenty years later, when it seemed that war would break out at any minute, he decided to revise the song. Kate Smith, a famous singer, sang it on a radio program. People loved the song, and it has been an American favorite ever since.

"God Bless America"

by Irving Berlin

God bless America,

Land that I love,

Stand beside her and guide her

Through the night with a light from above.

From the mountains, to the prairies,

To the oceans white with foam,

God bless America,

My home sweet home.

Character Traits

A character trait is something people show by the way they act. A person who keeps trying shows patience, and patience is a character trait.

Character traits are also called "life skills." Life skills can help you do your best, and doing your best leads to reaching your goals.

Sequoyah
Patience
Sequoyah showed patience by working for 12 years to create a Cherokee alphabet.

Martin Luther King, Jr.
Liberty
Martin Luther King, Jr. worked for fair treatment and liberty for all people.

Honesty is telling the truth and not cheating.

People who show **dependability** are people who do what they say they will. You can count on them to get a job done.

Liberty is freedom. People who work for liberty want to be free from the control of others.

Trustworthiness means a person can be trusted. A trustworthy person does not cheat, lie, or steal.

People who have **honor** are honest. They do what is right and good.

Acting with **civility** means having good manners. It means showing respect for others even if you do not agree with them.

Patience means being calm when facing hard problems. It also means keeping at a task even if it takes a long time.

Compassion is understanding and caring about other people's problems. Helping others is a sign of compassion.

Good sportsmanship means playing with a good attitude. It means not bragging if you win or complaining if you lose.

Geographic Terms

forest
a large area of land where many trees grow

hill
a raised mass of land, smaller than a mountain

▲ **desert**
a dry area where few plants grow

▲ **island**
land with water all around it

lake
a body of water with land all around it

mountains

hill

river

lake

ocean

mountain

a steep mass of land, much higher than the surrounding country

▲ **ocean**

a salty body of water covering a large area of the earth

peninsula

land that sticks out into water

plain

a broad, flat area of land

plateau

an area of flat land that is higher than the land around it

river

a large stream of water that runs into a lake, ocean, or another river

valley

low land between mountains or hills

valley

peninsula

plain

Atlas

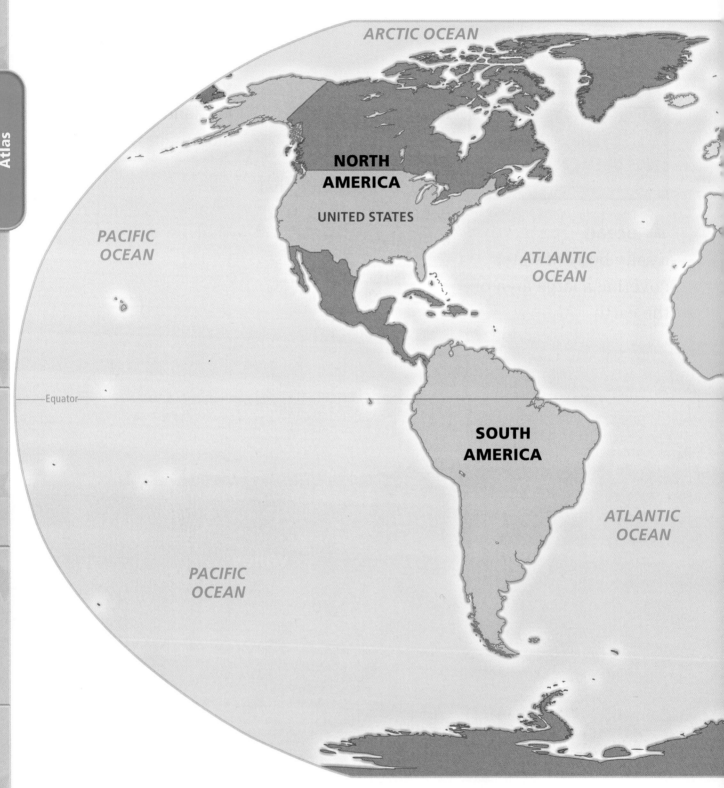

ARCTIC OCEAN

NORTH
AMERICA

UNITED STATES

PACIFIC
OCEAN

ATLANTIC
OCEAN

Equator

SOUTH
AMERICA

ATLANTIC
OCEAN

PACIFIC
OCEAN

Atlas

ARCTIC OCEAN

EUROPE

ASIA

PACIFIC OCEAN

AFRICA

Equator

INDIAN OCEAN

AUSTRALIA

North
NW   NE
West   East
SW   SE
South

Scale at Equator
0   1,000   2,000 kilometers
0   1,000   2,000 miles

ANTARCTICA

The World: Physical

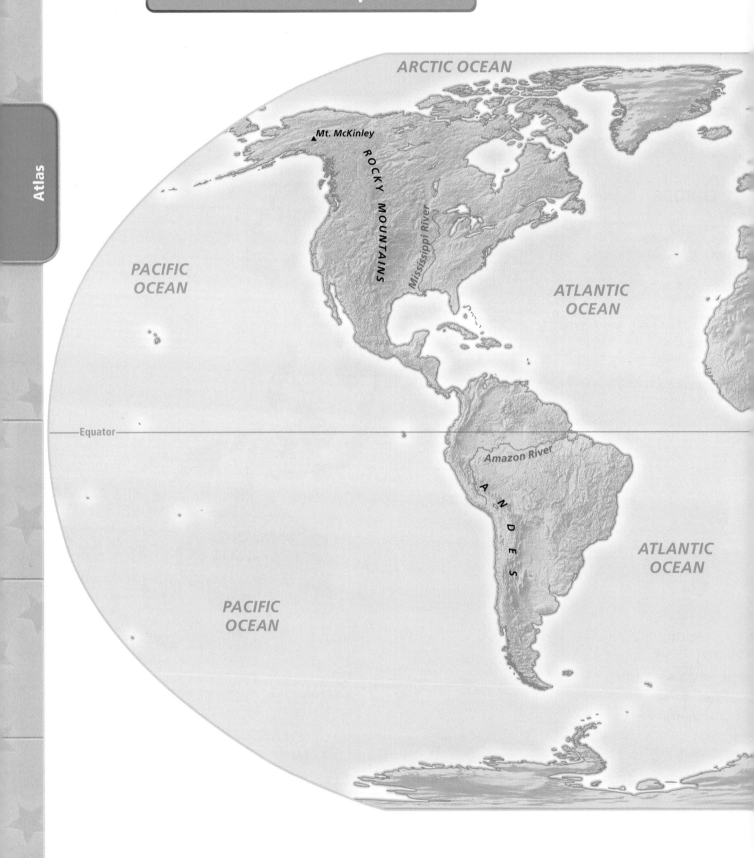

ARCTIC OCEAN

Mt. McKinley

ROCKY MOUNTAINS

Mississippi River

PACIFIC OCEAN

ATLANTIC OCEAN

Equator

Amazon River

A N D E S

ATLANTIC OCEAN

PACIFIC OCEAN

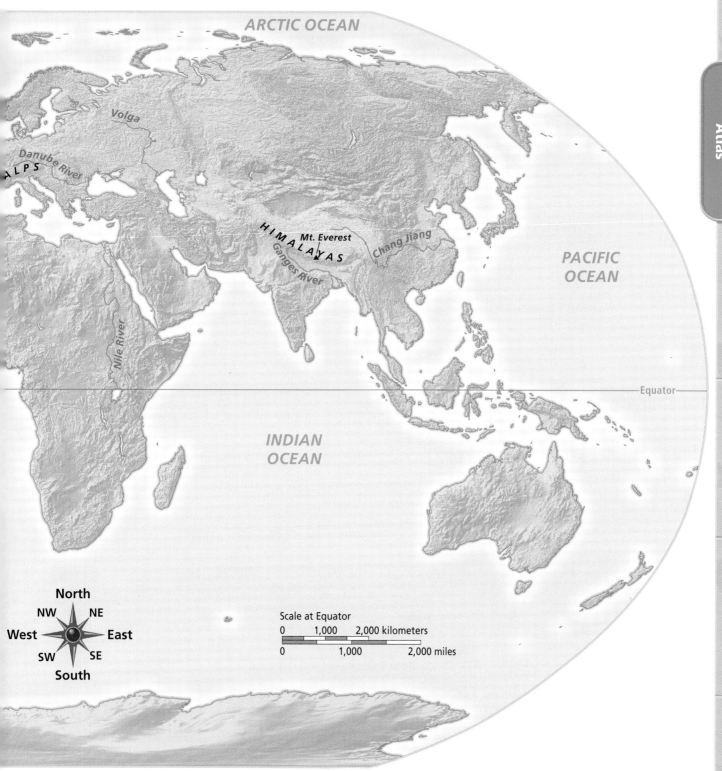

ARCTIC OCEAN

Volga

Danube River

ALPS

Nile River

HIMALAYAS

Mt. Everest

Ganges River

Chang Jiang

PACIFIC OCEAN

Equator

INDIAN OCEAN

North
NW   NE
West   East
SW   SE
South

Scale at Equator
0   1,000   2,000 kilometers
0   1,000   2,000 miles

North America

Atlas

North
NW   NE
West   East
SW   SE
South

PACIFIC OCEAN

HAWAII

Map Key
⊛   National Capital
—   National Boundary

0   400   800 kilometers
0   400   800 miles

ARCTIC OCEAN

GREENLAND

CANADA

Ottawa ✪

Washington, D.C. ✪

UNITED STATES

ATLANTIC OCEAN

Gulf of Mexico

BAHAMAS

Nassau ✪

DOMINICAN REPUBLIC

MEXICO

Havana ✪

CUBA

PUERTO RICO (U.S.)

Mexico City ✪

JAMAICA

Port-au-Prince ✪

Santo Domingo ✪

Belmopan ✪ — BELIZE

Kingston ✪

HAITI

Lesser Antilles

Caribbean Sea

Tegucigalpa ✪ — HONDURAS

Guatemala City ✪

GUATEMALA

San Salvador ✪

NICARAGUA

EL SALVADOR

Managua ✪

PANAMA

San Jose ✪

COSTA RICA

Panama ✪

The United States

ALASKA

0   500 kilometers
0   500 miles

WASHINGTON

OREGON

IDAHO

MONTANA

WYOMING

North
NW   NE
West   East
SW   SE
South

NEVADA

UTAH

COLORADO

CALIFORNIA

ARIZONA

NEW
MEXICO

Map Key

⊛ National Capital

—— National Boundary

—— State Boundary

HAWAII

0   200 kilometers
0   200 miles

NEW
HAMPSHIRE

VERMONT

MAINE

MASSACHUSETTS

NORTH
DAKOTA

MINNESOTA

NEW
YORK

RHODE
ISLAND

SOUTH
DAKOTA

WISCONSIN

MICHIGAN

CONNECTICUT

NEW
JERSEY

PENNSYLVANIA

IOWA

NEBRASKA

OHIO

DELAWARE

Washington, D.C.

ILLINOIS

INDIANA

WEST
VIRGINIA

MARYLAND

VIRGINIA

KANSAS

MISSOURI

KENTUCKY

NORTH
CAROLINA

TENNESSEE

OKLAHOMA

ARKANSAS

SOUTH
CAROLINA

ALABAMA

GEORGIA

MISSISSIPPI

TEXAS

LOUISIANA

FLORIDA

0   125   250 kilometers

0   125   250 miles

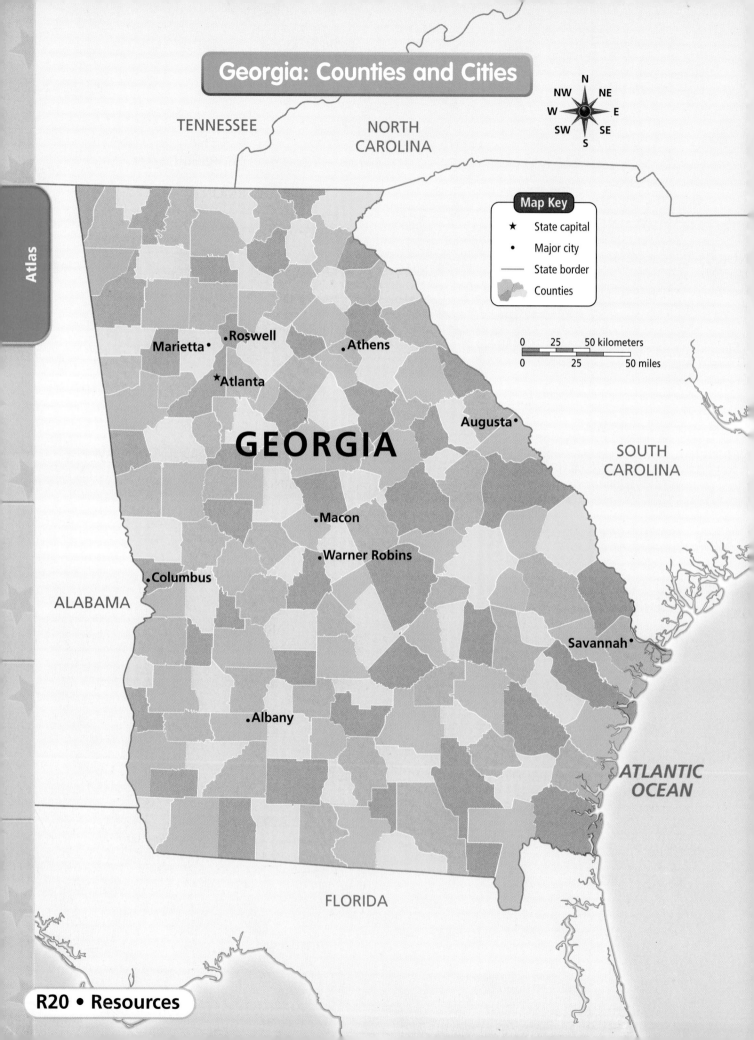

Georgia: Counties and Cities

TENNESSEE

NORTH CAROLINA

Map Key
★ State capital
• Major city
— State border
Counties

0   25   50 kilometers
0   25   50 miles

•Roswell
Marietta •
•Athens
★Atlanta
GEORGIA
Augusta•
SOUTH CAROLINA
•Macon
•Warner Robins
•Columbus
ALABAMA
Savannah•
•Albany
ATLANTIC OCEAN

FLORIDA

Atlas

Georgia: Land and Water

TENNESSEE

NORTH CAROLINA

Map Key

～～ River

▭ Water

🌱 Swamp

APPALACHIAN PLATEAU

BLUE RIDGE MOUNTAINS

APPALACHIAN MOUNTAINS

Chattooga River

N
NW   NE
W   E
SW   SE
S

Lake Sidney Lanier

Chattahoochee River

0   25   50 kilometers

0   25   50 miles

PIEDMONT

GEORGIA

SOUTH CAROLINA

Savannah River

Ocmulgee River

Oconee River

ALABAMA

Altamaha River

Flint River

Chattahoochee River

COASTAL PLAIN

ATLANTIC OCEAN

Okefenokee Swamp

St. Mary's River

FLORIDA

R21

Picture Glossary

A

ancestor

A family member who lived before you is an **ancestor.**
(p. 64) An **ancestor** of mine lived in China in the 1600s.

artifact

An **artifact** is an object made in the past. (p. 58) A tool, a bowl, or a pair of shoes can be an **artifact.**

B

bank

A **bank** is a safe place to keep money. (p. 151) Dad went to the **bank** to get money for gas.

barter

The exchange of goods or services without the use of money is called
barter. (p. 141) **Barter** takes place when you swap goods or services with someone.

benefit

A **benefit** is what you get when you make a choice. (p. 129) If you buy a game instead of a toy, the **benefit** is being able to play the game.

What I Get (Benefit)
Enjoy computer game today

bluff

A high place overlooking a river is a **bluff.** (p. 41) Savannah was built on a **bluff.**

Picture Glossary

capital

A **capital** is a city where the people in a government work. (p. 178) The **capital** of New Jersey is Trenton.

capitol

The building in which a state government meets is the **capitol.** (p. 177) Georgia's **capitol** building is in Atlanta.

ceremony

A **ceremony** is a formal act or series of acts done in honor of an event. (p. 32) A wedding is a **ceremony.**

citizen

A **citizen** is a person who belongs to a place. (p. 188) You are a **citizen** of the community where you live.

climate

The usual weather of a place over a long time is called **climate.** (p. 87) Southern Michigan has a **climate** with cold winters and warm summers.

coast

A **coast** is land next to a sea or an ocean. (p. 95) Georgia has a **coast** on the Atlantic Ocean.

colonist

A **colonist** is a person who lives in a colony. (p. 42) The **colonists** at Jamestown came from England.

colony

A **colony** is a place that is ruled by another country. (p. 39) England's first **colony** in North America was Jamestown.

communication

Any way of sharing information is **communication.** (p. 114) Newspapers and magazines are kinds of **communication.**

conflict

A **conflict** is a disagreement. (p. 186) Good citizens try to resolve **conflicts** peacefully.

Constitution

The **Constitution** is a plan for the government of the United States. (p. 202) The United States **Constitution** is more than 200 years old.

consumer

A **consumer** is someone who buys or uses goods or services. (p. 132) I am a **consumer** when I buy food at a store.

continent

A **continent** is a large body of land. (p. 80) The earth has seven **continents.**

county seat

The **county seat** is the town where county government meets and works. (p. 208) Americus is the **county seat** of Sumter County.

Sumter County

 D

democracy

A **democracy** is government by the people. (p. 203) People in a **democracy** choose their leaders.

detail

A **detail** is a small piece of information. (p. 102) Make sure you support your idea with **details.**

Main Idea
Details
1.
2.
3.
4.
5.

dictionary

A **dictionary** is a book that gives the meanings of words. (p. 156) Look up new words in a **dictionary.**

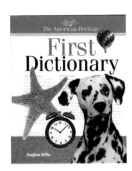

distance

The word **distance** means how far one point is from another. (p. 138) The **distance** across the table is 60 inches.

election

An **election** is a time when people vote. (p. 196) We have an **election** to choose a class president.

encyclopedia

An **encyclopedia** is a book or set of books that gives information about many topics. (p. 156) Look up a topic in an **encyclopedia** to find out more about it.

environment

The **environment** is the natural world around you. (p. 108) Land, water, plants, animals, and people are all part of the **environment.**

explorer

An **explorer** is a person who travels to find new things and places. (p. 38) Columbus was an **explorer** who traveled to the Americas.

fact

A **fact** is something that is true. (p. 174) A book about farms has many **facts** in it.

factory

A **factory** is a place where goods are made. (p. 140) It would be fun to go to a sneaker **factory.**

goods

Things people make or grow are called **goods.** (p. 140) Goods are things such as trucks and apples.

government

A group of people who work together to run a community, state, or country make up a **government.** (p. 168) Some people in our **government** work at city hall.

governor

The leader of a state's government is a **governor.** (p. 197) Georgia's **governor** serves for four years at a time.

grid

A **grid** is a pattern of lines that form boxes. (p. 68) A **grid** helps you find places on a map.

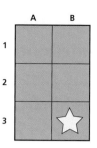

history

Everything people can know about the past is called **history.** (p. 30) You can read about **history** in books.

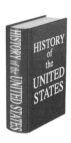

income

The money people earn when they work is called **income.** (p. 134) My mother uses her **income** to pay for our food.

independence

Independence means freedom from the rule of another nation. (p. 168) The 13 colonies wanted **independence** from Britain.

intermediate directions

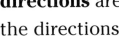

Intermediate directions are the directions in between north, east, south, and west. (p. 84) Northeast, southeast, southwest, and northwest are **intermediate directions.**

invention

An **invention** is something new that someone makes or thinks of. (p. 114) Thomas Edison thought of many important **inventions.**

justice

Justice means fairness. (p. 203) A good judge treats everyone with **justice.**

landform

A **landform** is one of the shapes of land found on the earth. (p. 94) A mountain is a **landform.**

law

A rule that everyone in a community, state, or nation must follow is called a **law.** (p. 191) A driver who does not stop at a stop sign is breaking a **law.**

liberty

The word **liberty** means freedom. (p. 203) The **Liberty** Bell is a symbol of our nation's freedom.

location

A **location** is a place. (p. 68) An airplane symbol may mark the **location** of an airport on a map.

main idea

The most important thought in a piece of writing is called a **main idea.** (p. 102) The **main idea** on that page is that people have many kinds of pets.

mayor

The leader of a city's government is a **mayor.** (p. 197) The **mayor** of Atlanta serves for four years at a time.

mountain

A **mountain** is a high land with steep sides. (p. 50) Brasstown Bald **Mountain** is the highest point in Georgia.

nation

A **nation** is a country. (p. 79) Canada is a **nation** to the north of the United States.

natural resource

Something in nature that people use is a **natural resource.** (p. 104) Water is an important **natural resource.**

needs

Things that people must have to live are called **needs.** (p. 128) Our **needs** are food, water, clothing, and shelter.

northeast

The direction between north and east is called **northeast.** (p. 84) New York City is **northeast** of Trenton, New Jersey.

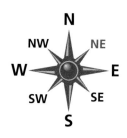

northwest

The direction between north and west is called **northwest.** (p. 84) Montgomery, Alabama is **northwest** of Tallahassee, Florida.

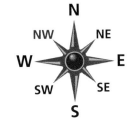

opinion

An **opinion** is a belief based on what you think or feel, rather than on facts. (p. 174) In my **opinion,** soccer is better than baseball.

opportunity cost

An **opportunity cost** is what you give up when you make a choice. (p. 129) If you buy a game instead of a puzzle, the **opportunity cost** is that you cannot play with the puzzle.

What I Give Up (Opportunity Cost)
Play with puzzle today

plateau

A **plateau** is an area of fairly flat high land. (p. 97) The Appalachian **Plateau** is one of Georgia's five regions.

president

A **president** is the leader of a nation. (p. 197) John Adams was the second **President** of the United States.

price

The amount of money you pay to buy something is called **price.** (p. 150) The **price** of a pencil is 15 cents.

BASIC PENCILS (without erasers)

15¢

primary source

A **primary source** is information from a person who was there. (p. 118) A **primary source** can also be an artifact.

producer

A **producer** is a person who makes or grows something. (p. 132) A baker is a **producer** of bread and rolls.

reed

A **reed** is the main stem from tall grass plants. (p. 53) The Cherokee used **reeds** in building their homes.

region

A region is an area that has some shared natural or human feature that sets it apart from other areas. (p. 94) The state of Iowa is in a plains **region.**

responsibility

A **responsibility** is something that you should do. (p. 190) Everyone has the **responsibility** to obey school rules.

ridge

A **ridge** is a long, narrow strip of high land. (p. 98) The Blue **Ridge** Mountains are in northeastern Georgia.

right

A **right** is something you are free to do. (p. 189) You have the **right** to speak freely.

river

A **river** is a large body of moving water that flows into a lake, an ocean, or another body of water. (p. 31) **Rivers** form parts of Georgia's borders.

sapling

A **sapling** is a young tree. (p. 53) The Cherokee used **saplings** in building their homes.

savings account

A **savings account** is a service from a bank that allows people to earn interest on their money. (p. 152) Aki's **savings account** earned 11 cents in interest last month.

scale

A line with a series of marks used to find distance on a map is a **scale.** (p. 138) Use a map **scale** to find how far apart two places are.

scarcity

Not having enough resources to meet people's unlimited wants is called **scarcity.** (p. 142) Because of **scarcity,** people must make choices in what to make or grow.

secondary source

A **secondary source** is information from a person who was not there. (p. 118) The lesson on inventions is a **secondary source.**

service

An activity that people do to help other people is called a **service.** (p. 141) A dentist provides a **service.**

settlement

A **settlement** is a small community started by people from another land. (p. 39) Savannah was the first English **settlement** in Georgia.

shelter

Something that protects or covers is called a **shelter.** (p. 128) Houses are kinds of **shelter.**

southeast

The direction between south and east is called **southeast.** (p. 84) Springfield, Illinois, is **southeast** of Des Moines, Iowa.

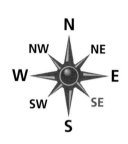

southwest

The direction between south and west is called **southwest.** (p. 84) Frankfort, Kentucky, is **southwest** of Columbus, Ohio.

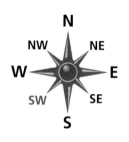

state

Part of a country is called a **state.** (p. 79) Georgia is one **state** of the fifty in the United States.

table

A **table** is a chart that puts information in order. (p. 148) A **table** has columns and rows.

Georgia Products	
Food	Other
Peanut butter	Rugs and carpets
Canned fruits	Chemical products
Baked goods	Electrical equipment
Chicken	Paper products

tax

A **tax** is money that a government collects from citizens and businesses. (p. 181) Georgia's government collects a **tax** on things such as baseballs and bats.

timeline

A **timeline** is an ordered group of words and dates that show when events happened. (p. 48) A **timeline** must be divided into equal parts.

Dan's Life History

Dan was born   Dan learned to read   Dan today

transportation

Any way of moving things or people from one place to another is called **transportation.** (p. 112) Cars are one kind of **transportation.**

valley

The low land between mountains or hills is called a **valley.** (p. 50) A **valley** often has a river running through it.

vote

To **vote** means to show or make a choice for a leader or a law. (p. 196) You may **vote** for class president or team captain.

wants

Things that people would like to have, but do not have to have to stay alive are called **wants.** (p. 128) A new bike and in-line skates are on my list of **wants.**

weather

What the air is like outside at any given time is called **weather.** (p. 86) Today the **weather** is warm and rainy.

Index

Page numbers with *m* after them refer to maps.

Index

Index

Index

Services

Index

Acknowledgments

For each of the selections listed below, grateful acknowledgment is made for permission to excerpt and/or reprint original or copyrighted material, as follows:

Permissioned Material

"God Bless America," by Irving Berlin. © Copyright 1938, 1939, © copyright renewed 1965, 1966 by Irving Berlin. © Copyright assigned to the Trustees of the God Bless America Fund. International Copyright Secured. All Rights Reserved. Reprinted by permission of the Irving Berlin Music Company.

Excerpt from "North" ("The Young Woman and the Thunder Beings"), from *Between Earth & Sky: Legends of Native American Sacred Places,* by Joseph Bruchac. Text copyright © 1996 by Joseph Bruchac. Reprinted by permission of Harcourt, Inc. and Barbara S. Kouts Agency.

Excerpt from "South" ("A Cherokee Legend"), from *Between Earth & Sky: Legends of Native American Sacred Places,* by Joseph Bruchac. Copyright © 1996 by Joseph Bruchac. Reprinted by permission of Harcourt, Inc. and Barbara S. Kouts Agency.

Maps

Maps.com
All cartographic maps done by Ortelious Design

Illustration Credits

36–37 Nenad Jakesevic. 68 Bob Depew. 85 Mark and Rosemary Jarman. 86 Mark and Rosemary Jarman. 90–93 Richard Cowdrey. 102 Jeffrey Mangiat. 116–117 Kathryn Mitter. 130–131 Doris Barrette. 141 Lisa Campbell Ernst. 156 Peter Richardson. 158 Anthony Lewis. 167 Viviana Diaz. 190 Kathi Ember. 191 Ron Berg. 198 Christiane Beauregard. 212 (b) Nathan Jarvis.

Photography

6 ©Ed Jackson. 7 ©Joseph Sohm/CORBIS. 8 ©HMCo./Ken Karp. 9 ©Dennis MacDonald/Photo Edit. 11 ©Keren Su/CORBIS. 13 The Granger Collection, New York. 23 Atlanta Skyline Panorama©www.slrobertson.com. 24 (bl) ©Ed Jackson. (br) ©Lynn McMeans. 25 (bl) National Portrait Gallery, Smithsonian Institution, Washington D.C./Art Resource NY. (bc) Hulton Archive/Getty Images. (br) ©CORBIS. (cr) ©Wally McNamee/CORBIS. 26–27 (c) ©Kevin Fleming/CORBIS. 28 (cl) ©Ed Jackson. (cr) ©Bettmann/CORBIS. 29 (cl) Maryann and Bryan Hempill/IndexStock. (br) Courtesy of Aparna Agrawal. 30–31 (b) Marilyn "Angel" Wynn/Nativestock.com. 32 (b) Marilyn "Angel" Wynn/Nativestock.com. (tl) Marilyn "Angel" Wynn/Nativestock.com. (tr) Marilyn "Angel" Wynn/Nativestock.com. 33 Marilyn "Angel" Wynn/Nativestock.com. 34 Marilyn "Angel" Wynn/Nativestock.com. 35 (tc) Ed Reschke/Peter Arnold, Inc. (tl) ©Hal Horwitz/CORBIS. (tr) ©imagebroker/Alamy. 38 John Anderson/Animals Animals/Earth Scenes. 40 The Granger Collection, New York. 41 The Granger Collection, New York. 42 ©Ed Jackson. 43 The Granger Collection, New York. 44 ©Ed Jackson. 45 ©Ed Jackson. 46 (b) ©Ed Jackson. (tr) ©Ed Jackson. 47 (b) ©Corpus Christi College, Oxford, UK/Bridgeman Art Library. (c) ©Ed Jackson. (b) ©Ed Jackson. (b) ©Lynn McMeans. (b) North Wind Picture Archives. (b) The Granger Collection, New York. (b) ©Dave G. Houser/CORBIS. 48 (tr) Myrleen Ferguson Cate/Photo Edit. (br) Burke/Triolo/Retrofile. 49 (bl) ©Horace Bristol/CORBIS. (bc) ©Claudia Kunin/CORBIS. (br) ©Don Mason/CORBIS. 50–51 ©David Munch/CORBIS. 52 ©William A. Bake/CORBIS. 53 (bl) Marilyn "Angel" Wynn/Nativestock.com. (br) Marilyn "Angel" Wynn/Nativestock.com. 54 (bl) Marilyn "Angel" Wynn/Nativestock.com. (tr) ©Layne Kennedy/CORBIS. Marilyn "Angel" Wynn/Nativestock.com. 56–57 (b) Donovan Reese/Panoramic Images. 57 (tr) ABPL Image Library/

Animals Animals/Earth Scenes. 59 Marilyn "Angel" Wynn/Nativestock.com. 60 Marilyn "Angel" Wynn/Nativestock.com. 61 Getty Images. 63 The Granger Collection, New York. 64 (cl) ©Lawrence Migdale. (br) ©Lawrence Migdale. 65 Muscogee (Creek) Nation Mound Building–Photo Courtesy of the Muscogee (Creek) Nation. 66 Library of Congress. 67 Courtesy of the Georgia Department of Economic Development. 70 (tl) Marilyn "Angel" Wynn/Nativestock.com. (tcr) The Granger Collection, New York. (tr) The Granger Collection, New York. 72 (tl) ©Jim Craigmyle/CORBIS. (tc) Bob Thomas/Stone/Getty Images. (tr) Image State Pictor/Picture Quest. 74–75 (c) Palmer Kane Studios. (c) Jesse Kalisher Gallery/Superstock. 77 (cl) ©David Muench/CORBIS. (cr) Dan Budnik/Woodfin Camp & Associates. 78 ©HMCo./Ken Karp. 79 ©HMCo./Ken Karp. 82 ©Karen Su/CORBIS. 83 (tr) ©HMCo. (b) ©HMCo./Ken Karp. 88 (cr) ©Johnny Crawford/The Image Works. (cl) Brad Wrobleski/Masterfile. 89 Alan and Sandy Carey/Photodisc Green/Getty Images. 90–91 Richard Cowdrey. 92–93 Richard Cowdrey. 96 Atlanta Skyline Panorama©www.slrobertson.com. 97 Courtesy of Georgia Department of Economic Development. 98 Courtesy of the Georgia Department of Economic Development. 99 Courtesy of Georgia Department of Economic Development. 100 Marilyn "Angel" Wynn/Nativestock.com. 101 (t) National Portrait Gallery, Smithsonian Institution, Washington D.C./Art Resource NY. (bl) National Portrait Gallery, Smithsonian Institution/Art Resource. (bl) Marilyn "Angel" Wynn/Nativestock.com. 104 International Stock/ImageState. 107 ©Vince Streano/CORBIS. 108 ©Collart HERVE/CORBIS. 109 (tr) Gibson Stock Photography. (tl) Gibson Stock Photography. 110 Cheryl Clegg/Index Stock Imagery. 111 ©Kevin Flemming/CORBIS. 112 Fine Art Photographic Library, London/Art Resource, NY. 113 ©George Hall/CORBIS. 114 (bl) ©Underwood & Underwood/CORBIS. (br) AP/Wide World Photos. 115 (tr) ©Royalty-free/CORBIS. (tl) ©Annie Griffiths Belt/CORBIS. 116 Kathryn Mitter. 117 (cl) Kathryn Mitter. (cr) Kathryn Mitter. 119 Library of Congress, Manuscript Division. 124–125 (c) David Young–Wolff/Photo Edit. 126 (cl) Ed Lallo/Index Stock Imagery. (br) Robert W. Ginn/Photo Edit. 127 ©HMCo./Ken Karp. 128 Frank Siteman/Index Stock Imagery. 129 SuperStock. 132 Photodisc/Getty Images. 133 ©LWA–Dann Tardif/CORBIS. 134 (cl) ©Jose Luis Pelaez, Inc./CORBIS. (br) Ed Lallo/Index Stock Imagery. 135 (tr) Comstock Images. (cl) Stone/Getty Images. 136 Hulton Archive/Getty Images. 137 (t) ©Bettmann/CORBIS. (bl) Hulton Archive/Getty Images. (bl) AP/Wide World Photos. 140 Rogério Reis/Tyba Brazil Photo. 141 ©CORBIS. 142 ©Michael Newman/Photo Edit. 144 (cr) Photo Researchers. (bc) Scott Barrow/ImageState. 145 (tc) Albert Gustaf Aristeded Edelfelt/SuperStock. (cr) Photodisc/Getty Images. 146 (tl) AP/Wide World Photos. (c) Photodisc/Getty Images. (cr) Photodisc/Getty Images. 147 (tl) ©Goldberg Diego/CORBIS. (tr) ©Goldberg Diego/CORBIS. 150 ©HMCo./Ken Karp. 151 (tl) John Coletti/Index Stock Imagery. (tr) Steve Cole/Photodisc/Getty Images. (tr) Stone/Getty Images. (cl) ©Walter Hodges/CORBIS. (cr) HMCo./C Squared Studios/Photodisc/Getty Images. 152 Steve Dunwell/Index Stock Imagery. 153 Wonderfile. 154 ©HMCo./Ken Karp. 155 ©HMCo./Ken Karp. 158 Anthony Lewis. 162–163 Ariel Skelley/Masterfile. 164 Hisham Ibrahim/Photographer's Choice/Getty Images. 165 Photodisc/Getty Images. 167 (tr) Viviana Diaz. (bl) Viviana Diaz. (br) Viviana Diaz. 168 Courtesy Don Troiani, Historical Military Imagebank. 170 ©Bettmann/CORBIS. 171 New York Historical Society/The Bridgeman Art Library. 172 Photo Edit. 173 (tl) Massachusetts Historical Society. (c) ©HMCo./Angela Coppola. 175 (cl) ©Museum of the City of New York/

CORBIS. (c) ©Bettmann/CORBIS. (cr) ©Bettmann/CORBIS. (frame) ©HMCo./Image Farm. 176 (cr) ©Paul Colangelo/CORBIS. 177 ©Dennis MacDonald/Photo Edit. 178 ©HMCo./Angela Coppola. 180 Elena Rooraid/Photo Edit. 181 ©HMCo./Angela Coppola. 183 ©HMCo./Angela Coppola. 185 ©HMCo./Angela Coppola. 186 ©HMCo./Ken Karp. 187 ©HMCo./Ken Karp. 188 ©HMCo./Angela Coppola. 189 ©HMCo./Angela Coppola. 192 Bonnie Kamin/Photo Edit. 193 Jose Carillo/Photo Edit. 194 ©CORBIS. 195 (bl) ©Bettmann/CORBIS. (bl) ©Bettmann/CORBIS. 196 ©HMCo./Jade Albert. 197 (tr) AP/Wide World Photos. (cr) AP/Wide World Photos. (br) Bell/Folio Inc. 198 (cl) Steven Begleiter/ImageState. (cr) Jim and Mary Whitmer. 199 AP/Wide World Photos. 200 ©Wally McNamee/CORBIS. 201 (t) Getty Images. ©Hulton Archive/Getty Images. (b) Larry Fisher/Masterfile. 204 Peter Gridley/Taxi/Getty Images. 205 (tr) Doug Armand/Stone/Getty Images. (cl) Peter Gridley/Taxi/Getty Images. 206 ©Steve Chenn/CORBIS. 207 (tr) Richard Hutchings/Photo Edit. (bl) AP/Wide World Photos. 210 ©HMCo./Angela Coppola. 216 Francis Miller/Time Life Pictures/Getty Images. R8 (cl) National Portrait Gallery, Smithsonian Institution, Washington D.C./Art Resource NY. (br) ©CORBIS. R22 (bl) Steve Dunwell/Index Stock Imagery. (cl) Marilyn "Angel" Wynn/Nativestock.com. (tl) Courtesy of Aparna Agrawal. R23 (bcr) Maryann and Bryan Hempill/Index Stock Imagery. (tr) Alan and Sandy Carey/Photodisc Green/Getty Images. (bl) ©Tom & Dee McCarthy/CORBIS. (bcl) ©Claudia Kunin/CORBIS. (tcl) ©Dennis MacDonald/Photo Edit. R24 (bcr) ©Steve Chenn/CORBIS. (bl) ©HMCo./Ken Karp. (tcl) ©HMCo./Ken Karp. (tl) Jack Star/PhotoLink/Photodisc/Getty Images. R25 (br) Diaphor Agency/Index Stock Imagery. (tcr) The Bridgeman Art Library. (tr) New Moon/Panoramic Images. (bcl) ©HMCo./Jade Albert. R26 (cl) ©Paul Colangelo/CORBIS. (tl) Allan Davey/Masterfile. R27 (bcr) Leif Skoogfors/Woodfin Camp & Associates. (tcr) Ron Berg. (tr) Thomas Winz/Panoramic Images. (bl) David Young–Wolff/Stone/Getty Images. (cl) ©Bettmann/CORBIS. R28 (bcr) Robert W. Ginn/Photo Edit. (tcr) Taxi/Getty Images. (bl) ©David Munch/CORBIS. (cl) AP/Wide World Photos. R29 (br) ©HMCo./Ken Karp. (cr) ©Bettmann/CORBIS. R30 (br) ©HMCo./Angela Coppola. (tcr) ©HMCo./Ken Karp. (tr) Mark Heifner/Pan Stock/Picturequest. (bl) ©J. Schwanke/Alamy. (cl) ©Charles Gupton/CORBIS. R31 (br) ©CORBIS. (tr) ©Royalty-Free/CORBIS. (tcl) ©John G. Wilbanks/Alamy. R32 (br) ©Jim Craigmyle/CORBIS. (tl) Michael Melford/Imagebank/Getty Images. (br) Bob Thomas/Stone/Getty Images. (br) ImageState Pictor/PictureQuest. R33 (tr) ©HMCo./C Squared Studios/Photodisc/Getty Images. (bl) ©HMCo./Ken Karp. (cl) ©Joseph Sohm/CORBIS. (tl) ©Bettmann/CORBIS.